Every Wednesday Morning

Weekly Encouragement from the Bible and Beth

Beth Smith

Everything's gonna be okay, because God is in control.
Roy Farmer

For Bert, who typed and printed, cut and stapled,
and made it possible for me to share God's Word.

CONTENTS

Contents

Introduction

In the summer of 2001, Beth Smith began giving a weekly devotional to those seeking encouragement at the Between Jobs Ministry of North-West Bible Church in Spring, Texas. She has continued in that role for over 13 years. Every Wednesday morning, she awakens in the wee hours to review the lesson lovingly and prayerfully prepared during the previous week. Every listener receives both verbal inspiration and a hardcopy handout: a small card with verses or slogans and some sort of memento—a sticker, a coin, a candy or small toy. Those handouts, produced by her husband Bert, stay in pockets and purses long after the devotional has ended, serving as a reminder of the Biblical truths Beth teaches.

I am blessed to be Beth's daughter. These are my mom's devotionals, edited just enough to make her spoken words come alive in written form. They have inspired thousands through the Between Jobs Ministry, and are offered to you with the hope that they will warm your heart and draw you closer to Jesus. (And as a delightful sideline, you will get to know Beth better.)

My parents' handout material is provided at the back of this book. We hope that some of you will use this book to create handouts of your own and to share these devotionals in a group setting.

If you would like to contact Beth, you can reach her at: everywednesdaymorning@gmail.com, or write to her at:
Beth Smith, 4008 Louetta Road #283, Spring, Texas 77388-4405

—Brenda Koinis
Summer, 2016

A Note from Beth

How blessed I am to have grown up in the church! My earliest memories are of attending Vacation Bible School and singing in the children's choir in a red brick building in Norfolk, Virginia. My teen years in Shelby, North Carolina, were filled with choir, youth fellowship group, summer camp and a variety of Christian conferences. I even met the love of my life at church. After we moved to South Florida, we taught Sunday school, helped with youth groups, and attended services in a big white sanctuary less than a mile from our home.

Then God did a wonderful thing. A new teacher was assigned to our adult Sunday school class. Boy, could he talk about Jesus! Suddenly a whole new world opened up to me. I learned about my personal Savior, a Lord who loved me and offered forgiveness, grace, and new life. The Bible became easier to understand. Prayer became second nature to me. I vividly remember kneeling at the foot of my bed, alone in the house, surrendering my life to Jesus. Somehow I had missed the message of the gospel in all my years as a busy church-goer, yet those years had sown the seeds for this moment. Now Jesus was real to me and the center of my life. I belonged to him. The peace that passes all understanding surrounded me.

As time went on, I was privileged to hear many wonderful Christian speakers at conferences, camps, in our home, and in the homes of others. I filled my Bible with notes as I soaked up their teaching. I immersed myself in their books. My writing is, in many ways, the result of their instruction. God provided so many gifted pastors that, truth be told, I do not even remember all their names. I do remember their love for the Lord Jesus, and that the Holy Spirit planted their teaching into my life.

I pray that by the time you have read this book, you will be able to say with me, "Now I belong to Jesus!" I hope you'll join me in singing these words in your heart: "All to Jesus I surrender. All to Him I freely give. I will ever love and trust Him, in His presence daily live."[1]

—Beth Smith

chapter one

Pure Gold

M y husband took me to Alaska for my 75th birthday. Alaska!
Beautiful scenery! Great history! Friendly people! This place
was called Seward's Folly back when the United States purchased it from Russia for two cents an acre. That proved to be a tremen-
dous bargain. Alaskans are so proud of being the largest state that they
sell tee shirts displaying a map of Alaska surrounding a map of Texas.
The caption reads, "Isn't Texas cute?"

During our trip, I heard plenty of stories about the Alaskan gold
rush. Rich veins of gold were discovered, furiously mined, and quickly
depleted. Of course, gold is still mined in Alaska, but now it is done by
selling tourists a bucket of dirt and showing them how to pan for tiny
traces of gold. Everyone hopes to find a huge nugget like the one the
panning instructor wears around his neck. Rest assured, those tourists are
still helping to make gold mining profitable.

During the gold rush, some prospectors were fooled into thinking
that they'd found real gold, when all they'd really found was something
called iron pyrite, rocks with flecks of shiny material in them. These rocks
were worthless. Because so many were fooled, iron pyrite became known
as "fool's gold." I want you to know where our real gold is—where we
have a never ending supply of genuine gold—in the Word of God.

Remember the crippled beggar to whom Peter said, "*Silver and gold
have I none, but such as I have give I you. In the name of Jesus Christ of Nazareth, rise up and walk*" (Acts 3:6 KJV). What did the cripple do? He went
"*walking and leaping and praising God.*" He received far more than he asked

for. Would he have traded his healing for a truckload of gold coins? Of course not! Here's a bit more from the Bible regarding gold.

"The law from your mouth is more precious to me than thousands of pieces of silver and gold."

—Psalm 119:72

"I love your commandments more than gold, more than pure gold."

—Psalm 119:127

"Blessed are those who find wisdom, those who gain understanding, for she is more profitable than silver and yields better returns than gold."

—Proverbs 3:13-14

God has given us not just a few pieces of gold, but a never ending source of gold. The Bible, the Word of God, is a gold mine that will never stop producing ore.

Are you a bit timid about mining gold from the Bible? When Bert and I were first married, we knew we should read the Bible together. We'd read for a few nights, then realize we really didn't understand it. We found it intimidating—just too hard, so we'd stop. A few months later, we'd try again with much the same results. I know that over the years we changed, but we also got a translation of the Bible that was easier to understand than the King James Version we had been using. That made a big difference. If you don't have a modern or revised version, I recommend that you get one and try it out.

The King James Bible was authorized by King James 1 of England in 1604. While it was translated into the common language of the day, the words and phrases of the early seventeenth century are much different from the words we use today. The "thee's" and "thou's" and "eth's" and word arrangements can throw us off, interrupting our concentration. For example, here is John 14:10 from the King James Bible. *"Believest thou not that I am in the Father and the Father in me? The words that I speak unto you, I speak not of myself; but the Father that dwelleth in me, he doeth the works."*

Here's the same verse taken from the New International Version.

"Don't you believe that I am in the Father, and that the Father is in me? The words I say to you I do not speak on my own authority. Rather, it is the Father, living in me, who is doing the work."

Another important thing to remember as we go into our gold mine, the Bible, is that we do not go alone. John 14 says that the Holy Spirit will lead us into all truth. The Greek word for the Holy Spirit is *Paraclete*, which means "one who is called alongside to help." He will help us if we allow him to.

Many Bible readers have stories about the Holy Spirit directing them to a particular scripture at a particular time. For me, it was right before my husband was scheduled to have a cochlear implant, a bionic ear. Almost completely deaf, Bert had some hearing in one ear, very little really, and none in the other. The surgery needed to be done on the good ear to have the greatest chance of success. It was scary. If anything went wrong, Bert would be in complete silence.

We were sure God wanted him to have the surgery. There was no other answer, no hearing aid or other solution that would work for him. Bert was a prime candidate for the implant. He had a great doctor. He'd gotten encouragement from others who had received implants. Medicare would pay for it. Everything was positive, but it was still scary. Then the Holy Spirit stepped in and did his work.

I'm sure that over my life I must have read Psalm 94 more than once, but the week before the surgery, I read it in the New International Version (an older version than you might find on the shelves today). In verse 9, I found these exact words, *"Does he who implanted the ear not hear?"* No other version that we own used the word "implanted." Yes, I know that verse isn't about a man getting a cochlear implant; but my heavenly Father knew we needed encouragement, and he gave it. He'll do the same for you. The next time you hear a sermon or read a verse that makes you think, "I needed that," or, "That was for me," you can be sure it was God at work.

Our gold mine is filled with power for living in God's world, in God's way. Every time Jesus was tempted by Satan, he said, "It is written..." and quoted scripture. If Jesus needed to do that, then surely we do.

"All Scripture is inspired by God and is useful to teach us what is true and to make us realize what is wrong in our lives. It corrects us when we are wrong and teaches us to do what is right. God uses it to prepare and equip his people to do every good work."
—2 Timothy 3:16-17 NLT

It's time for us to think not "Thar's gold in them thar hills," but, "Thar's gold in this here Book." (It hurts me as an English teacher to write that way.) The Word of God doesn't offer fool's gold. It offers the real McCoy. So pull out your Bible and read on!

chapter two

A Stake in the Ground

There's a story told about a farmer who accepted Christ as his Savior. But whenever he had a mean thought, or argued with his wife, or was tempted to lie about something, he wondered if he really was a Christian. One day, as he plowed a field near his house, old doubts started to return. He stopped his tractor, got a huge fence post, walked to the center of the field and drove that stake into the ground. "There!" he said. "I have accepted Christ. I am a Christian here and now and forevermore." He got back on the tractor and continued his work. After that, whenever a doubt came into his mind or his spirit, he'd point at the stake and say, "I am a Christian. There's my stake. I have already made that decision."

Perhaps we each need to drive a stake of remembrance into the ground of our own faith. It may be that some of us have never driven the stake that says we are *new*. If we have driven that one, then we need to drive in one that reminds us that we are *being renewed* day to day by the power of God. Here's the proof:

> "To all who believed him and accepted him, he gave the right to become children of God. They are reborn—not with a physical birth resulting from human passion or plan, but a birth that comes from God."
> —John 1:12-13 NLT

What freedom comes to us with the truth in those two verses! When we accept Christ as Savior by believing that he is God's son and then rely on his death on the cross as payment for our sins, we become God's children. 'Ever heard comments like these?

- "Well, our family has always been stubborn."
- "He's just mean spirited like his daddy was."
- "You know alcoholism runs in her family."

No more of that! Because of Christ, we are no longer limited by our human nature, by our physical birth. As God's children, we can now be like our heavenly Father. I love this verse. "*If any person is in Christ, he is a new creation (a new creature altogether), the old (moral and spiritual condition) has passed away. Behold the fresh and the new has come*" (2 Corinthians 5:17 AMP).

I've already become a new creature in Christ by accepting him. If this old creature is a new creature, though, why do I sometimes act like the old creature? Why don't those of us who have experienced the new birth act like perfect beings – angelic, sweet, and obedient all the time? Let me be clear. When we become God's children, we are new. Our spirits are forever new. We are headed for heaven. But even though our spirits are right with God, we have minds, and wills and emotions that have to be brought in line with God's spirit in us.

How can what we think, what we want, and what we feel be submitted to God? That happens through a daily process of renewal. It's as if we have to get dressed in our new spirit every day. The Bible refers to it as putting off the old man and putting on the new.

"Since you have heard all about Him and have learned the truth that is in Jesus, throw off your old evil nature and your former way of life, which is rotten through and through, full of lust and deception."
—Ephesians 4:21-22 NLT

"Be constantly renewed in the spirit of your mind, having a fresh mental and spiritual attitude, and put on the new nature created in God's image in true righteousness and holiness."
—Ephesians 4:23-25 AMP

This daily renewal involves:

- Looking to Jesus for help.
- Losing sight of ourselves.
- Asking for forgiveness.
- Forgiving others.
- Loving others every day.
- Reading God's Word.
- Doing our best to be more like Jesus.

Will we fail to do all that? Certainly! But God always gives us the opportunity and the power to start afresh. Don't get discouraged. God's grace is enough. According to 2 Corinthians 12:9, his strength is made perfect in our weakness. Let's resolve to let Christ renew us every day by living for him. Let's put our stakes in the ground of faith as a reminder that we are being renewed every day by God's grace and power.

chapter three

A Different Diet

W e all have favorite foods. I'm partial to chocolate, not the fancy stuff, just the good ol' grocery store variety. I may love chocolate, but I want to love God's Word far more, to "eat" it more often than I do any variety of chocolate. I want to wear out my Bible. But hear me, while I want to do that, I have just as hard a time reading my Bible and studying God's Word as you do. I'd hate for you to know how many days I never get around to more than a quick read. Even so, here's how I want to feel about God's Word.

> *"I have esteemed and treasured the words of His mouth more than my necessary food."*
>
> —Job 23:12 AMP

> *"Your words were found, and I ate them; and Your words were to me a joy and the rejoicing of my heart."*
>
> —Jeremiah 15:16 AMP

> *"How sweet are Your words to my taste, sweeter than honey to my mouth!"*
>
> —Psalm 119:103 AMP

Why do we want that attitude? How do we know it's important? Matthew chapter 4 gives us an account of Jesus being tempted by the devil in the wilderness. Jesus fasted there for forty days and, having eaten nothing for such a long time, was hungry. The devil came to him and said, "*If you are really God's Son, then change these stones into bread.*" Jesus refused, saying, "*It is written: 'Man shall not live on bread alone, but on every word that comes from the mouth of God.'*" (Matthew 4:3-4).

If we are supposed to live by the Word, how can we do it? This is oh-so-easy to say, "Read God's Word, the Bible. Study it. Let it speak to us. Let it change us. Let it give us the life that God desires for us." Easy to say? Yes, indeed. So why is it so hard to do? I can describe two of the reasons: our flesh (our own selfish desires) and the devil. Think about these scenarios:

- We decide, "Yes, I am going to read the Bible. I'm setting aside a special time for study." Time comes. We're ready. Phone rings. Neighbor drops in. Toilet overflows. Whatever. The Devil.
- We read the Word, but we forget what it said. Snatched away. The Devil.
- We read the Word, and we remember what we read. (This is exciting!) Problems come up. We argue with our spouse. The Word gets crowded out. Flesh and the Devil.
- We read the Word. We enjoy it and feel lifted up. (We're very excited!) We're ready to read more. Then something we like comes on TV. The Astros are playing the Cubs, or our favorite movie is on TV. Sure, we almost know the movie by heart, but after all, it is our favorite. Flesh.
- Now I've gotten up early (like Jesus did). I'll read in the quiet. 'Good time to concentrate. 'Got my coffee or tea, pencil and notebook. I'm sure God will speak to me. I'm ready. "THUD!" I just heard the newspaper being delivered. Hmmm. I'll just check the ball scores, then the sales ads, then the business section. Flesh.

"Eating the Word" can be a struggle. Being a Christian is not for sissies. It's a battle. It's a good fight of faith. Here's the truth: we need to recognize the tricks of the Devil, we need to know our weak flesh, and we must be prepared to defeat them. The flesh and the Devil are no match for our Savior's power. We absolutely can triumph over them, and God is absolutely faithful to make a way for us. The flesh and the Devil may pacify us, but only God's word will satisfy us.

I'd like for you to read these next five Bible verses and think carefully about what they promise us. The Devil doesn't want you to know these truths.

- Jesus said, "*If you live in me and My words remain in you and continue to live in your hearts, ask whatever you will and it will be done for you*" (John 15:7 AMP).
- Jesus said, "*If anyone observes My teaching (lives in accordance with My message, keeps My word), he will by no means ever see and experience death*" (John 8:51 AMP).
- "*My comfort in my suffering is this: Your promise preserves my life.*" (Psalm 119:50).
- "*For everything that was written in the past was written to teach us, so that through the endurance taught in the Scriptures and the encouragement they provide we might have hope*" (Romans 15:4).
- "*The word of God is alive and powerful. It is sharper than the sharpest two-edged sword…It exposes our innermost thoughts and desires.*" (Hebrews 4:12 NLT). That sharp knife or sword belongs to the Holy Spirit who loves us and uses his power for our absolute best.

The Word is God's power for us. What we eat physically matters, but eating God's Word matters so much more. We can't treat the Bible like snack food—a quick bite here, a quick bite there. Reading the Bible without meditating on what we have read is like eating without chewing. You know, fads about eating correctly come and go. Protein. No carbs. Extra carbs. No meat. Yes, meat. No sugar. No fat. Low fat. It gets ridiculous. Thankfully, there will be never be a change in the "eating" of the Word. This food plan is forever.

Some people say you are what you eat. That's good news if we are on a steady diet of the Word of God. Reread the verses just discussed. Think on them. Meditate. Let the Holy Spirit use them in your life.

Consider posting them somewhere where you'll see them so that you won't forget what they teach.

Psalm 34:8 says, "*Taste and see that the Lord is good.*" Here's my paraphrase of that passage.

> *Chocolate is yummy.*
> *Sugar is sweet.*
> *But it's the Word of God*
> *We need to eat.*

chapter four

Happy Hearts

Will Rogers said, "We're all here for a spell, get all the laughs you can."[2] A sainted nun wrote in 1582, "From somber, serious, sullen saints, save us, O Lord."[3] And we've all heard stories about how laughter helped people overcome sickness or depression. The need for a happy heart is nothing new, though. The book of Proverbs has been teaching the importance of cheerfulness for thousands of years.

- Proverbs 17:22 says, "*A cheerful heart is good medicine, but a crushed spirit dries up the bones.*" We want to have happy hearts and cheerful minds.
  Proverbs 15:15 (AMP) teaches that, "*All the days of the desponding and afflicted are made evil by anxious thoughts and forebodings, but he who has a glad heart has a continual feast regardless of circumstances.*" How can we go from having anxious hearts, expecting bad and harmful things to happen, to having a glad heart and a continual feast regardless of circumstances? Jesus gives us a big part of the answer to that question in Luke, chapter 10.

Jesus sent some of his followers to go ahead of him into the towns that he planned to visit. They went, and when they came back to Jesus they were filled with joy. They said, "*Even the demons submit to us in your name.*" (v.17 AMP). Can't you just see them laughing and talking about their successes? I imagine they were very happy.

Jesus knew his disciples' circumstances wouldn't always be happy and joyful. He knew his own death was coming, and that his followers would be confused, discouraged, and eventually would suffer many things. So Jesus said, in verse 20 (AMP), "*Do not rejoice at this, that the spirits are subject to you, but rejoice that your names are recorded in heaven.*" The most important reason for rejoicing, for having a happy heart, is our citizenship in heaven, bought for us by Jesus Christ. That's a real cause for joy!

My husband Bert and I were on a bus tour once and, as folks do on such trips, we spent some time with other passengers getting acquainted. A common question was, "What do you do?" or "What did you do before you retired?" One nicely dressed, personable man answered, "Well, I'm still employed. When I am working, I wear a dress and sell the ultimate fire insurance." He was an Episcopal priest! We laughed, of course, but we have even greater cause to have a merry heart if we have that insurance he was talking about.

Consider this ad in an old newspaper. "Lost: Dog with three legs, blind in left eye, missing right ear, tail broken. Answers to the name 'Lucky.'" Even if we seem to be in as bad a shape as that dog, we don't live by luck. We live by faith, faith in the God of the Universe, faith in the God who has done and can do all things. That faith produces a glad heart no matter what our circumstances may be.

Jesus also tells us in John, chapters 15 and 16, that the things he asks us to do are for this purpose: *That our joy may be full.* How do we get that fullness of joy? For starters, we can remember that the most important reason for rejoicing, for having a happy heart, is our citizenship in heaven—bought for us by Jesus Christ. What else is characteristic of a glad or merry heart? Let me make a few suggestions.

- Such a heart is full of forgiveness, forgiveness received from God for sin and given quickly to everyone else. No heart full of resentment and unforgiveness can be happy. On the other hand, "*Oh, what joy for those whose disobedience is forgiven, whose sin is put out of sight!*" (Psalm 32:1 NLT).

- A happy heart regularly and sincerely counts blessings and thanks God for them. The Bible tells us to *"Give thanks to him and praise his name"* (Psalm 100:4).
- A glad and merry heart is full of trust. It knows God is in control and allows him to lead. Psalm 32:10 (AMP) tells us that, *"Many are the sorrows of the wicked, but he who trusts in and relies on the Lord shall be surrounded with compassion and loving-kindness."*
- A glad heart is also quick to obey. Acts 5:29 (AMP) recounts the apostles saying, even under threat of punishment, *"We must obey God rather than men."*

No heart is perfect, but aiming toward forgiveness, thankfulness, trust, and obedience will put us on the right path to the glad and merry heart God offers us. There's an old hymn that gives us great instruction. It says, "Trust and obey, for there's no other way to be happy in Jesus, but to trust and obey."[4]

Let's begin to smile more, to even let our glad hearts lead us to laughter. No, laughter won't get us a job, heal a marriage, or solve any of the problems we face. Nevertheless, we can have a happy heart with God's blessing. No matter what our circumstances, he wants us to be full of joy.

chapter five

Mustard Seeds

few years ago, all my grandchildren were wearing WWJD jewelry. The initials stood for the question, "What would Jesus do?" Over fifty years ago, teenagers, including me, were wearing mustard seed jewelry. It was usually a single seed in a clear plastic ball (like a charm) attached to a chain on a bracelet or necklace. You were really in style if you had one! It came with a card that had Matthew 17:20 printed on it. Jesus said, *"If you have faith as small as a mustard seed, you can say to this mountain, 'Move from here to there,' and it will move. Nothing will be impossible for you."*

Well, personally, I didn't move any mountains, but the mustard seed and the verse did help me learn that faith is important and powerful. Faith was a rather vague concept for me. I grew up thinking if things went well, I had faith. If things didn't go well, it was my fault for just not having enough faith. Believe me, that is far from the truth. *The Amplified Bible* adds these words to describe faith, "Faith is trust and confidence that springs from our belief in God." Maybe you're thinking, "I guess I just don't have faith." Well, if you've accepted Christ as your Savior, you do. The Bible says in Ephesians 2:8, *"For it is by grace you have been saved, through faith."* Don't get a big head about having enough faith to accept Christ. It was, after all, God's grace that gave you the faith to believe.

Let me put it this way: if you go out for breakfast in the Deep South, you're likely to get a huge serving of white grainy stuff on the side. No matter what you order, you'll see that pile of white. For those of you who are Yankees, I'll explain. Those are grits, and grits come with everything. Let me tell you – grace comes with everything, and everything, including our faith, comes by grace. In Hebrews 11:1 (KJV), faith is defined in this way. *"Faith is the substance of things hoped for, the evidence of things not seen."* This tells us two things about faith.

- Faith is so real that it's called a substance. The Greek word for faith used in that verse means "that which stands under something to provide a base." So faith is the foundation of what we hope for.
- Faith is the proof or evidence of the existence of unseen things. Faith deals with the invisible.

2 Corinthians 5:7 says, *"For we live by faith, not by sight."* The New Living Translation puts it this way, *"We live by believing and not by seeing."* The world says, "Seeing is believing." The spiritual world says just the opposite. First we must believe, then we will see.

Can we ever be truly content trying to live only in the physical world, the world we can see with our own eyes? I don't think so. God has designed us to live in his spiritual and eternal world. Faith is what connects us to the unseen realities of God's world. Our aim, our goal, is to trust God and his Word without demanding any other evidence. Wow! Wouldn't that be great! So, how do we stay in faith? How can we stand firm in our beliefs? How does faith come?

"Faith comes by hearing, and hearing by the word of God" (Romans 10:17 KJV). When we really know who God is, we can believe. We find out who he is by reading his Word. So, what shall we do with our mustard seeds of faith? Let's root them in God's love.

In Ephesians 3:17, Paul prays, *"That Christ may dwell in your hearts through faith. And I pray that you, being rooted and established in love…"*

In Matthew 14:28-31, Peter walked on water, but then he felt the wind, became frightened, and he began to sink. Jesus reached out and saved him, saying, "Oh you of little faith. Why did you doubt?"

Faith or doubt? We waver for the same reasons that Peter did. We forget who God is and what he is like. If only we could really get a hold on how much he loves us. He loves us, not our works or achievements, us! God loves us because he is love. The Bible tells us he knew us before the foundation of the earth. He loved us before we loved him. He loves us all the time, and nothing can separate us from that love. When we believe that, our faith will be firm, and it will grow. That tiny mustard seed, under good conditions, will grow higher than a man can reach. Our faith, rooted in God's love, established through reading his Word and based upon his grace, can grow large as well. Jesus said nothing will be impossible for us if we have faith even as small as a mustard seed.

chapter six

The Very Best Valentine

My husband Bert and I just celebrated our 59th wedding anniversary. As you can imagine, we've had our good times and our hard times; but, believe me, if you just hang in there the good times get better and better. People often ask us the secret of our long and happy marriage. It's really quite simple. Two evenings every week, we take time to go out to a restaurant. A quiet dinner – soft music – some candlelight – a slow drive home. Two evenings a week. He goes on Tuesdays and I go on Fridays. No, not really. The truth is that we've learned to love and appreciate one another through thick and thin.

So, Happy Valentine's Day! I want to remind you that God sent us the greatest Valentine, Jesus Christ, because he loves us so much. 1 John 4:15-16 says,

"If anyone acknowledges that Jesus is the Son of God, God lives in them and they in God. And so we know and rely on the love God has for us. God is love. Whoever lives in love lives in God, and God in them."

The fact that God is love explains a lot. Love is his nature. That's why he can love us when we're unlovable. Wouldn't it be terrible to have to strive constantly to make God love us, trying to do enough to be acceptable to him, to be loved by him? We can rely on his love for us, even though we don't deserve it.

Not only is God love, but his love for us is eternal. Romans 8:35-39 (NLT) says,

"Can anything ever separate us from Christ's love? Does it mean he no longer loves us if we have trouble or calamity, or are persecuted, or hungry, or destitute, or in danger, or threatened with death? (As the Scriptures say, 'For your sake we are killed every day; we are being slaughtered like sheep.') No, despite all these things, overwhelming victory is ours through Christ, who loved us. And I am convinced that nothing can ever separate us from God's love. Neither death nor life, neither angels nor demons, neither our fears for today nor our worries about tomorrow—not even the powers of hell can separate us from God's love. No power in the sky above or in the earth below—indeed, nothing in all creation will ever be able to separate us from the love of God that is revealed in Christ Jesus our Lord. Who shall separate us from the love of Christ? Shall trouble or hardship or persecution or famine or nakedness or danger or sword?...No, in all these things we are more than conquerors through him who loved us. For I am convinced that neither death nor life, neither angels nor demons, neither the present nor the future...nor anything else in all creation will be able to separate us from the love of God that is in Christ Jesus our Lord."

God is love. His love is eternal. And he has asked us to love each other. In John 13:34-35, Jesus said,

"A new command I give you: Love one another. As I have loved you, so you must love one another. By this everyone will know that you are my disciples, if you love one another."

Let's think about loving in three ways: thought, word, and deed.

Thought: If we dwell on someone's faults or shortcomings, we'll have a mighty hard time showing them love. It's better to believe the best of every person. And aren't we thankful that God doesn't keep a list of our offenses? We aren't to keep a list either. *"Love bears up under anything and everything that comes, is ever ready to believe the best of every person"* (1 Corinthians 13:7 AMP).

Word: After we practice thinking good things about others, we need to speak them—good things, complimentary things. We can almost always find (even if we have to search for it) a good, encouraging, or positive word to speak to those around us. *"Kind words are like honey—sweet to the soul and healthy for the body"* (Proverbs 16:24 NLT). We can bite our tongues when sharp words are trying to make their way out of our mouths. The old kid's chant, "Sticks and stones may break my bones, but words will never hurt me" is a lie. Most of us can remember some sort of terrible thing said to us in childhood that still hurts. God wants us to love with our words.

Deeds: Once we are thinking and speaking love, it's easier to move on to loving in our actions, showing our love and the love of God in what we do. *"Dear children, let us not love with words or speech but with actions and in truth"* (1 John 3:18).

Where do we begin? What are we going to do in the name of love? For each of us the action we take will be different, but here are a few suggestions. (I'm making them to myself as well as to you.)

- Forgive someone. (God has forgiven us, and we need to do the same.)
- Show real kindness. (We have the power to be kind to others.)
- Do for others. (Call a friend, do a chore that isn't yours, or meet a need even if it's inconvenient.)
- Be generous with your hugs and compliments. Don't just say, "That color looks nice on you." Say, "Wow! That color really makes your eyes sparkle."

We all know how to love. Now we just need to do it, and extravagantly. The word extravagant is usually associated with money, but the truth is that we need to be extravagant with our love toward others, because God has been extravagant with his love toward us. Let's share that love every day.

chapter seven

Love Muscles

O n our 41st wedding anniversary, our daughter Becky gave Bert and me a book called *365 Ways to Kiss Your Love*. Some of the suggestions are creative, some sweet, some silly, and some are downright embarrassing, but the book does remind us that kissing is important. One page suggested setting a timer and making one kiss last a whole minute.

When I was a teenager, if your date kissed you goodnight, you were going steady. Times have changed. The word love is tossed around far more casually these days. Sometimes I think we've forgotten what true love is, but we can learn plenty about true love from the Bible.

At the end of the twelfth chapter of 1 Corinthians, Paul wrote that we should desire the highest and best and most helpful gifts from God. Then he said that the best gift, the best way of living, is love. This love is not some mushy, worked up, pretend, or temporary love. It's real, and if you know Jesus as your Savior, you already have the kind of love we're going to explore today. I know that's true, because Romans 5:5 tells us, *"God's love has been poured out into our hearts by the Holy Spirit."* It's poured in. It's there. All we have to do is use it, exercise it. I want to consider five areas (and there are many more) where we can exercise God's love, five love muscles we need to use. These come from 1 Corinthians 13:4-5.

If you want to make these five love muscles easy to remember, grab a pen and paper. Trace your hand the way you did when you were going to draw a Thanksgiving turkey in kindergarten. Be sure your drawing has a thumb and four fingers. Ready? Here goes.

- *Love is patient.* How can we exercise this love muscle? We could stop being in such a hurry all of the time. We could stop and listen to someone else's ideas for a change, or be willing to be uncomfortable in a situation and still keep a good attitude. Grocery store check-out lines are a place where I need to practice patience. Write PATIENT on one of the fingers in the outline you've drawn.

- *Love is kind.* Kindness is a lost art in our modern world. Simply being nice makes such a difference. What exercises can we do here? Pick up someone else's mess. Help fix dinner. Turn off the computer or the TV to listen to our mate, our children or our friends. (Just pushing the mute button doesn't count.) Write KIND on another outlined finger.

- *Love is not jealous or self-seeking.* Jesus said we should lose sight of ourselves and our own interests. That's so hard to do, especially in tough times. But we can do it by deliberately encouraging and blessing others. Call someone. Send an email, telling them you care. Help physically. Give what you can. If, every day, we would think, "Who can we bless today?" our bent toward self-centeredness would be cured. Write ENCOURAGING on another finger.

- *Love is not boastful or proud.* That means love is humble. That's not a very popular attribute today. Jesus is our great example of humility. He went from the throne of heaven to a manger and then to a cross. What can we do? Serve others. Look to give instead of to get. This should be especially true in our homes. Sometimes that's the hardest place to exercise humility. Write HUMBLE on another finger.

- *Love keeps no record of wrongs.* Love forgives. We need to remember how many times God has forgiven us, and then go and do the same to others. What should we do when we are offended? Just drop it. Let it go. Write FORGIVING on the last digit.

22

Exercising love isn't always easy, but it is doable. By keeping our eyes on Christ and on what true love is, we can succeed. Consider reading 1 Corinthians 13 every day this week. It's a life changer. Of course, we won't always succeed. Some time ago I had the opportunity to practice what I preach. I needed to exercise a particular love muscle, but didn't want to do it. It really stretched me physically and emotionally. I did do it, though.

Afterwards, my daughter asked me how it went. She could see that I wasn't feeling good about the good I had done, and that I was about to give a pitiful answer. I was going to tell her that I was uncomfortable. I feared I had said the wrong thing in the wrong way. Before I could speak, though, my daughter said, "Mom, give me your hand, fist closed, palm up." One by one, she unfolded my fingers as she said, "You did it for him." True love is to do whatever we do as unto Jesus with open hands.

Look at the hand you've drawn and the five things we want to practice doing. We can be patient and kind and encouraging and humble and forgiving. The more we exercise these muscles, the stronger they'll become. When we feel weak about loving, when we don't want to exercise love muscles, we can still do it for Jesus' sake. That will be the best love muscle-building exercise ever.

chapter eight

What Color is Your Tongue?

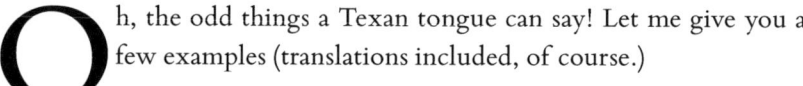h, the odd things a Texan tongue can say! Let me give you a few examples (translations included, of course.)

- "The engine's running, but ain't nobody driving" means the person in question isn't too smart.
- "He's tighter than bark on a tree" is just a creative way of saying someone's stingy.
- A Texan might describe a chatterbox this way, "She's got enough tongue for ten rows of teeth."
- And "This is not my first rodeo" is code for "I've been around."

Our tongues can be sweet or sour, powerful, and unpredictable. When I was a kid, jawbreakers were made of layers and layers of different colors. As we sucked on them, we would open our mouths, stick out our tongues and ask, "What color is my tongue now?" Before long, the color would change.

Our tongues often do need to change, not their color, but the way we use them, what we say about ourselves and about our circumstances. We naturally say with our mouths what we think in our minds and believe in our hearts. Too often, we limit ourselves by our thoughts and our words. We fail to accept ourselves for who God says we are in Christ. Here's just a sample of what God says about us:

- We are children of God. "*Yet to all who believed him and accepted him, he gave the right to become children of God*" (John 1:12 NLT).
- We are members of Christ's body. "*Now you are the body of Christ, and each one of you is a part of it*" (1 Corinthians 12:27).
- We are forgiven. "*He forgave us all our sins, having canceled the charge of our legal indebtedness, which stood against us and condemned us*" (Colossians 2:13-14).
- We serve a God who will take care of all our needs. "*And this same God who takes care of me will supply all your needs from his glorious riches, which have been given to us in Christ Jesus*" (Philippians 4:19 NLT).
- We have all the wisdom we need when we ask God for it. "*If any of you lacks wisdom, you should ask God, who gives generously to all without finding fault, and it will be given to you*" (James 1:5).
- We are never alone. God has said, "*Never will I leave you; never will I forsake you*" (Hebrews 13:5).

Studying those verses, writing them down and even saying them out loud, can do great things for you. It can increase your faith. Romans 10:17 tells us that, "*Faith comes from hearing the message, and the message is heard through the word about Christ.*" Having faith will affect how we live, what we think about our circumstances, and what our tongues say.

What do you say about yourself, whether out loud or within your mind? We might as well admit it: sometimes we call ourselves awful things. We'd never let other people talk to us the way we talk to ourselves. That's called our "inner dialogue." In order to change a negative inner dialogue to a positive one, we must first ask ourselves, "Is what we're saying true—really true?" An even better question is, "Do we believe the Bible is true?" If so, we can change the color of our tongues, not with candy, but with God's Word. Once we accept the things God has said about us in his Word, we can begin to speak his confidence into our own lives.

I challenge each of us to believe the truth from God and to speak that truth. We've all tried many other ways to find peace, joy and faith. Why not see if this helps? It will. Believing we can live victorious Christian lives doesn't take any more effort than believing we can't. If God said it, if he promised it, let's take it as truth. Let's speak it out loud. A change of our tongues will mean a change in our lives.

How do I know this? Well, let's just say, "This ain't my first rodeo."

chapter nine

Out of Control

I once saw a bumper sticker that said, "If God is your co-pilot, you're sitting in the wrong seat." There's a lot of truth to that, don't you think? Still, we like control. When someone comes up with an idea, we often say, "Well, that's okay, but have you considered...?" When my spouse asks me to do something, I almost always think of a reason to do it a different way—my way. This type of attitude makes surrendering our lives to God difficult.

When are we most likely to give up our control? When we have needs we can't possibly meet on our own. That's when God teaches us dependence on him. And that's a glorious, wonderful thing. Needs are the stuff from which miracles are made. When our needs merge with faith in God and commitment to him, the way is open for God to work. Of course, before we're able to surrender to him, we need to believe he has the power to accomplish what he promises.

There's an account of terrible disbelief in the Old Testament (Numbers 14). Having been miraculously brought out of Egypt, the Israelites were led by Moses to the border of Canaan, the land God had promised to them. God told Moses to send in twelve spies to look at the country and size up the situation. When the twelve returned, all of them praised the country, saying that it was a land flowing with milk and honey. "But," they reported, "the people of the land are huge, and their cities are well fortified."

Ten of the spies said, "We can't conquer these people. They're like giants. We are as grasshoppers compared to them." Two of the twelve,

Joshua and Caleb, held a different opinion. Caleb said, "Let's take the land. We're well able to conquer it, because the Lord is with us. Fear not!"

Caleb and Joshua saw the situation differently because they remembered God's promise to give them Canaan. Sadly, though, the Israelites chickened out. They didn't go into Canaan, so God allowed them to wander around in the desert for forty years until a whole new generation was born and reached adulthood. Of the original group brought out of Egypt, only Caleb and Joshua entered the Promised Land. That speaks volumes to us about believing what God says.

When we lean on our own power, thinking we are in control, what blessings we forfeit! We're limited by our own problems and circumstances. On the other hand, when we surrender to God, when we allow him to be in control, he uses our circumstances for good, to draw us closer to him.

My husband Bert had the most deadly type of melanoma removed from his back in 1965. It was a "get your affairs in order" diagnosis, and the doctor's only comfort to me was that Bert would not suffer long. Death would come quickly. Fortunately, we had become Christians about a year before and belonged to a group of dedicated believers who prayed with and for us. One day, a dear elderly lady said, "Beth, as you pray for Bert, you're praying like a child who wants her father to tie her shoes for her but won't let go of the laces. You really must let go and let God be in control."

When I did surrender Bert and the whole situation to God, I cannot describe the peace that came. What a blessing to release my husband to a loving, heavenly Father, trusting him no matter what the outcome! Fifty years later, Bert is still with me, but I know that he could have died. Once I surrendered control, I knew that a different outcome would have been all right too. God's promise is that *"in all things God works for the good of those who love him, who have been called according to his purpose"* (Romans 8:28).

We're often facing at least one kind of distressing situation—illness, unemployment, wayward children, difficult decisions. These things that trouble us are a reminder that, when life is hard or confusing, we can still smile, because we believe God is all powerful, all knowing and all loving. We can give him control, letting him work in us and for us.

My pastor once taught me a strange word, "egbokbegiic." Pronounced like "egg-bok-bee-geek," it's an acronym for "Everything's gonna be OK because God is in control." If you're tired, frustrated, or worried, just remember that funny word and all it represents.

Go ahead and lose control of yourself to God. He is loving and good. He is worthy of our trust. Egbokbegiic.

chapter ten

Double-Minded

Today, I want to discuss the word "double." There are double plays in baseball. You can enjoy a double dip ice cream cone or be double jointed. Do you remember Dubble Bubble Gum? You might have to double back on a highway because you are lost. (Well, women would double back, but men always keep going, claiming, "There'll be a crossover to the right road just ahead.") And, please don't tell my no-cards-allowed uncle, but I even know you can double down when you play blackjack.

I knew a man from my husband's home church in Elizabeth City, North Carolina. His name was Mr. H. Every time he was asked to pray in Sunday school or church, he always said, "Lord, give us a double portion of your holy blessing." Everyone would chuckle a bit. Mr. and Mrs. H., being unable to have children, had adopted a child. Later Mrs. H. gave birth to two sets of twins within four years. That was truly a double portion!

However, we can also be double-minded. That's a "double" phrase we want to strictly avoid.

Here's what James 1:5-8 says

"If any of you lacks wisdom, you should ask God, who gives generously to all without finding fault, and it will be given to you. But when you ask, you must believe and not doubt, because the one who doubts is like a wave of the sea, blown and tossed by the wind. That person should not expect to receive anything from the Lord. Such a person is double-minded and unstable in all they do."

I believe God loves us and wants to bless us with our hearts' desires, but we block him by being double-minded. James writes that we should not be like a wave tossed by the winds. Tossed by the wind might sound like this:

- "Lord, I am praying to you. Are you really listening, God? Are you even there?"
- "Yes, of course you listen, God, I know you love me, but why aren't you answering me?"
- "Oh, God, I know you have a plan for my life. What if it isn't a plan I like?"
- "Lord, I want whatever you want. No, not completely. I'm afraid of your plan. You might send me to Africa to become a missionary."
- "You are the Lord of all my life, but right now I need to stop praying and plan my day."
- "By the way, Lord, I need focus and wisdom."

The question is, how can we overcome being double-minded? The answer is to set our own minds. Setting our minds and keeping them set will take some practice, but that's what the Bible tells us to do.

"Those who live according to the fleshly nature set their minds and pursue those things which gratify the flesh. But those who live according to the Holy Spirit set their minds on and seek those things which gratify the Spirit."

—Romans 8:5 AMP

"Set your minds and keep them set on what is above (the higher things), not on the things that are on earth"

—Colossians 3:2 AMP

I want to suggest two things to help us start setting our minds.

First of all, let's set our minds on God and who he is – remembering what we already know about him and getting to know him better

31

through Bible study and prayer. As we do this, something exciting happens. We begin to say what God says, and we get our minds off ourselves. When we pray, focusing God instead of ourselves, we start moving from being pitiful to being powerful, because we are operating in God's power, not our own.

- "Nobody loves me" changes to "God loves me."
- "I am so alone" becomes "God will never leave me."
- "I have nothing to hold on to" is replaced by "God is my Rock and my Fortress."
- "There's nothing good in my life" is disproved as we learn that God is good.
- "I'll never amount to anything" gives way to knowing that Christ makes us a new creation.

The second half of setting our minds, overcoming double-mindedness, is a perpetual homework assignment, something we must practice every day. In Philippians 4:8-9 (NLT), Paul writes: "*And now, dear brothers and sisters, one final thing. Fix your thoughts* (set your mind) *on what is true, and honorable, and right, and pure, and lovely, and admirable. Think about things that are excellent and worthy of praise. Keep putting into practice all you learned and received from me—everything you heard from me and saw me doing. Then the God of peace will be with you.*"

I pray we will be able to set our minds on things above, on God and on the blessings that he provides. The only "double" word now is to ourselves. I double-dare us to practice these truths. I know, if we do, we will be doubly blessed.

chapter eleven

A Joyful Noise

- Psalm 51:15 says, "*Open my lips, Lord, and my mouth will declare your praise.*"
- In Psalm 63:3-5, we find, "*Because your love is better than life, my lips will glorify you…with singing lips my mouth will praise you.*"

There are times in our lives when we need to make some noise—joyful noise! For those of us who aren't musically gifted, our singing qualifies as joyful noise. Psalm 100 is a powerful encouragement to praise the Lord.

> "*Shout for joy to the Lord, all the earth. Worship the Lord with gladness; come before him with joyful songs. Know that the Lord is God. It is he who made us, and we are his; we are his people, the sheep of his pasture. Enter his gates with thanksgiving and his courts with praise; give thanks to him and praise his name. For the Lord is good and his love endures forever; his faithfulness continues through all generations.*"

That sounds great, but maybe the person who wrote that had many things for which to be thankful. How can we praise God, or make a joyful noise, when we aren't feeling well, when we're in trouble, or when we have a whole slew of problems coming against us? Is it even important to praise him then? Let me tell you a story. It's found in 2 Chronicles, Chapter 20.

King Jehoshaphat of Judah was a rich and powerful man. He was highly esteemed by his countrymen. He didn't worship false gods, but sought the true God and obeyed his commands. The Bible says he was, "committed to the ways of the Lord." He made his share of mistakes, of course, but at the time of this story he had turned again to the Lord. He'd even traveled around his country encouraging the people to return to the Lord God of their ancestors.

One day a group of messengers came and warned Jehoshaphat that a great army, one formed by the alliance of three separate groups, was coming to attack Judah. That vast army was coming to destroy him, and there was no way he could win such a battle. It was hopeless. Have we ever felt like this? We've been doing our best, and suddenly disaster strikes. What do we do about it? Here's what Jehoshaphat did. He sought the Lord for guidance and ordered a national fast to show that he and his people were serious about seeking God. All the people came together to seek the Lord. As they prayed, Jehoshaphat reminded himself and all his people of the nature of their God. He recalled what God had done for them in the past. He affirmed their faith. Praying in that way built up his faith. We need to remind ourselves of the promises and the power of our loving heavenly Father, especially in dark, difficult times.

God sent his Spirit upon one of the men in the crowd, and he spoke these words:

> *"Listen, King Jehoshaphat and all who live in Judah and Jerusalem! This is what the Lord says to you: 'Do not be afraid or discouraged because of this vast army. For the battle is not yours, but God's.'"*
> —2 Chronicles 20:15

He goes on to tell them where to find the enemy and where to take up their positions against them, but he also says,

> *"Stand firm and see the deliverance the Lord will give you, Judah and Jerusalem. Do not be afraid; do not be discouraged. Go out to face them tomorrow, and the Lord will be with you"*
> —2 Chronicles 20:17

Then the king and all the people bowed down with their faces to the ground and worshipped God. Worshipping God is a good way of surrendering our problems to him.

The next morning as King Jehoshaphat assembled the army, he appointed singers (joyful noise-makers) to walk in the front. They sang to the Lord, a sure and humble sign of belief in what God had promised. They sang, *"Give thanks to the Lord, for his love endures forever"* (verse 21). Do you think all his people felt like making that joyful noise? Surely some were afraid. Some may have doubted. Some may have felt like running the other way. But listen to the next verse. It's the real point of today's lesson, the power of praise.

> *"At the very moment they began to sing and give praise, the Lord caused the armies of Ammon, Moab, and Mount Seir to start fighting among themselves. The armies of Moab and Ammon turned against their allies from Mount Seir and killed every one of them. After they had destroyed the army of Seir, they began attacking each other."*
> —2 Chronicles 22-23 NLT

What might happen in our own lives if we decided to bow down, worship God, and believe what he says? Right now, some of us are saying, "I already do that." If so, then what about the next step? Praise him, make a joyful noise to him, all the time, not just when things are going well, not just when we feel like it.

"Through Jesus, therefore, let us continually offer to God a sacrifice of praise— the fruit of lips that openly profess his name" (Hebrews 13:15). If things aren't going well, if we don't feel like praising God, it almost seems fake to do it. No! No! The Bible says to praise God at all times, especially when we don't want to. That's what makes it a sacrifice. If we desire God's spiritual power working in our lives, we need to take our positions, in the front of the line, where we make a joyful noise of praise. Let's get to shouting, "Give thanks to the Lord, for his love endures forever." Let's remember that as King Jehoshaphat and his people began to sing and praise, God went into action on their behalf.

Let's be reminded by every song we hear this week, that we've been called upon to make a joyful noise. If we get discouraged, may our lips still shout out "Hallelujah," (which means "Praise God") as we trust him to take us through every difficulty.

Let's get noisy!

chapter twelve

No More Excuses

I once heard a preacher say, "An excuse is a reason wrapped up in a lie." Are you as good at finding excuses for your actions, or lack of action, as I am? If we were face-to-face today, I'd hand you a Dum Dum lollipop right now as a visual reminder that most excuses are just plain dumb, especially if we're telling them to God.

This excuse habit isn't new. Let me give you a few examples from the Bible. Even though these people went on to obey, their first reactions were excuses.

In chapter 6 of Judges, the Israelites were in deep trouble (again). They were being starved to death by the Midianites. God called Gideon to the rescue, addressing him as a mighty man of fearless courage. Gideon answered with an excuse, *"But Lord, how can I rescue Israel? My clan is the weakest in the whole tribe of Manasseh and I am the least in my entire family"* (Judges 6:15 NLT). We do that, don't we? We tell God we can't do what he asks because we're just nobodies. We don't come from a very good background. We're not well educated. We're the poorest of the poor. In other words, we tell God he's not able to use us.

God called Jeremiah to be a prophet to the Israelites, saying to him, *"I knew you before I formed you in your mother's womb. Before you were born, I set you apart and appointed you as my spokesman to the world"* (Jeremiah 1:5 NLT). Wow, that would inspire and convince anyone, right? Nope. Jeremiah's first response was an excuse. "I can't speak for you. I'm too young." Does that excuse sound familiar? Sometimes we think we're too young and inexperienced or (as in my case) too old and worn out. That's just a flimsy excuse if we've been called by God to act.

In the book of Exodus, God even spoke from a burning bush, assigning Moses the task of going to Pharaoh and leading the Israelites out of Egypt. Moses immediately offered two excuses: They won't believe me, and I'm not a good speaker. Do we dare to tell God that we don't have the talents or skills to do what he wants us to do?

Jesus told a parable about a man who prepared a great feast. When everything was ready he sent servants to notify his guests that it was time for them to come. Sadly, they all began to make excuses.

- "I've bought a field, and I have to go see it."
- "I've just bought five pair of oxen, and I need to try them out."
- "I've just gotten married, so I can't come."

Our excuses for not doing what God wants us to do aren't so very different from theirs.

- "I'm too busy with my family."
- "I'm overloaded with work."
- "I have to take care of my responsibilities or my possessions."
- "I have other plans."

In the light of God's power and God's grace, we stand without excuse for our disobedience.

How do we break our habit of making excuses? Try starting here. Do the last thing you remember thinking God wanted you to do, but that you didn't do. Perhaps it's something that offers a great challenge. Maybe it's something as simple as writing a letter or making a phone call. We may think we can't go through with whatever those things are, but God's Word tells us that:

- He knows us.
- He has empowered us with his Holy Spirit.
- He never leaves us or forsakes us.

- We can do anything he asks us to do, because he will make
  us able.

I heard a story about a group of Marines who were using war games for training. Instead of using weapons, the men were told to use verbal cues. For example, when they "fired" their unloaded rifles, they were to say "Bang! Bang!" They said "Boom" when lobbing an imaginary grenade.

A young soldier spotted a member of the enemy team, but all of his shouts of "Bang!" and "Boom!" did nothing. The other soldier simply held his ground. When asked for an explanation, the unmovable Marine simply said, "Rumble, Rumble! I'm a tank!"[5]

With Christ we're tanks. Next time we're about to offer excuses for avoiding what we know we should do, we could say to ourselves, "Rumble! Rumble!" Then move forward and do it. Write "Rumble! Rumble!" someplace where you can see it this week. Let those words remind you that we can do anything God wants us to do through Christ who gives us strength.

chapter thirteen

No More Foolishness

Reverend Henry Ward Beecher, a clergyman in the late 1800's, is said to have entered Plymouth Church one Sunday morning, only to find that a letter addressed to him had been left on the pulpit. He opened it and read the single word "Fool." Quietly and with great seriousness, he told the congregation about the letter and then said, "I have known many an instance of a man writing a letter and forgetting to sign his name, but this is the only instance I have ever known of a man signing his name but forgetting to write the letter."

What do you think of when you hear the word "fool"? Perhaps the song "Why Do Fools Fall in Love?" comes to mind. Maybe you think of familiar sayings like these. "He played the fool." "He was taken for a fool." "That was a foolhardy thing to do." I heard this one a number of times in my youth, "Cut out that foolishness!"

I wondered if the Bible had anything to say about this subject, and was amazed to find twenty-three references about fools and twenty-six containing the word foolish or foolishness. Here are a few highlights.

- *"Fools despise wisdom and instruction"* (Proverbs 1:7).
- *"Fools hate knowledge"* (Proverbs 1:22).
- *"The mouth of a fool feeds on folly"* (Proverbs 15:14).
- *"A fool's heart blurts out folly"* (Proverbs 12:23).

The greatest folly that fools blurt out is found in the first verse of Psalm 14 and again in Psalm 53, *"The fool says in his heart, 'There is no God.'"*

It seems to me that the opposite of foolishness is wisdom. In my concordance, there are thirty-two references to wise or wiser and twenty-nine to wisdom. Surely this must be something God wants us to understand. Here are just four scriptures I want to share about wisdom.

- *"Reverence for the Lord is the foundation of true wisdom. The rewards of wisdom come to all who obey him"* (Psalm 111:10 NLT).
- *"How much better to get wisdom than gold, and good judgement than silver"* (Proverbs 16:16 NLT). That's the opposite of what the world teaches us, isn't it?
- *"To acquire wisdom is to love yourself; people who cherish understanding will prosper* (Proverbs 19:8 NLT). Isn't that good news!
- *"Through skillful and Godly wisdom is a house (a life, a home, a family) built, and by understanding it is established (on a sound and good foundation)"* (Proverbs 24:3 AMP).

These verses make me want to be a wise person. The question is, how do we get wisdom instead of becoming fools? James 1:5 tells us that if we are lacking wisdom we should ask God to supply it, because he gives generously to all. He's already given us his wisdom. Do you know where? In his Word, the Bible. How foolish we are when we don't read it! He gave it to us.

Here's another question. How will we recognize Godly wisdom when we get it? Here's what James 3:17 (NLT) says,

"But the wisdom from above is first of all pure. It is also peace loving, gentle at all times, and willing to yield to others. It is full of mercy and the fruit of good deeds. It shows no favoritism and is always sincere."

Those are real goals to hold up for our lives. If we want to be wise, we must be:

- peace loving
- gentle
- considerate

41

- merciful
- impartial
- full of good deeds

Can we really be all these things? No, not by our willpower, determination, talents or abilities. We simply can't become wise on our own. So, how can we? Who will help us? We are told by 1 Corinthians 1:24 that, "*to those whom God has called, both Jews and Greeks, Christ is the power of God and the wisdom of God.*" Our only hope for Biblical wisdom lies in our relationship with God through Christ.

The characteristics of a truly wise person are all found in Christ. When we're seeking wisdom, we're really seeking to be like Christ. Not many years ago, kids were saying, "I want to be like Mike." (Michael Jordan, of course. We knew exactly what they meant.) Now we say, "I want to be like Christ." To do that, we have to know him. To know him we must read his Word (his wise instructions) and do what we find there, thus living wisely.

Let's not be foolish! Let's get wisdom by following Christ.

chapter fourteen

F.R.O.G.

Today I want to use the word F.R.O.G. to discuss our relationship to God. F. R. O. G. is an acronym that stands for Fully Rely On God. As you read the definition of *rely*, think about our relationship with God. What does rely mean?

- To have confidence and trust.
- To have assurance that one will not be let down by another.
- To be assured of support.
- To depend on confidently based on past experiences.

That's what the dictionary says. What does the Bible have to say about relying? First some don'ts. Don't rely on:

- The law. None of us can obey it all. (Romans 2:17-24)
- Our own strength. We're too weak to help ourselves. (Proverbs 28:26)
- Gold or money or wealth. It doesn't last. (Psalm 49:16-17)

We can't rely on unfaithful people, either. Proverbs 25:19 (NLT) warns that, "*Putting confidence in an unreliable person in times of trouble is like chewing with a broken tooth or walking on a lame foot.*" That's painfully descriptive, isn't it? So where can we put our confidence? On whom can we rely?

- Psalm 65:5 reminds us that God is *"our Savior, the hope of all the ends of the earth and of the farthest seas."*
- Proverbs 14:26 (AMP) promises that, *"In the reverent and worshipful fear of the Lord there is strong confidence, and His children shall always have a place of refuge."*
- Ephesians 3:12 declares that *"we may approach God with freedom and confidence."* We can be sure God won't turn us away.

When we have problems and pain, or when our worldly needs seem to press in on us from every side, we can forget to put our confidence in God. We get discouraged, and discouragement can cause mental and spiritual dementia. It affects our perception, our memory, and our judgment. It reduces our ability to remember who God is, how he loves us, and what he has done for us in the past.

We need to deliberately remember the things he has done. It's even a good idea to write them down so we can see them, letting them move from our memory, to a pen and paper, to our eyes and finally to our hearts.

To rely on God is also to trust Him, to have faith in Him. What is faith? Many of you may know Hebrews 11:1 by heart. Here it is from *The Amplified Bible.* *"Now faith is the assurance (the confirmation, the title deed) of the things we hope for, the proof of things we do not see, and the conviction of their reality — faith perceiving as real fact what is not revealed to the senses."*

The New International Version puts it this way, *"Now faith is confidence in what we hope for and assurance about what we do not see."*

The whole eleventh chapter of Hebrews describes people who walked and lived by faith, not by sight. It is a wonderful, powerful description of F. R. O. G. – fully relying on God. I hope you'll take the time to read it in its entirety.

Finally, to rely means to depend on someone for support and aid. Can we depend on God for help? Absolutely, and here's the proof:

- *"Let us then approach God's throne of grace with confidence, so that we may receive mercy and find grace to help us in our time of need"* (Hebrews 4:16).

- *"We wait in hope for the Lord; he is our help and our shield"* (Psalm 33:20).
- The Lord is *"my help and my deliverer"* (Psalm 40:17).
- *"God is our refuge and our strength, an ever-present help in trouble"* (Psalm 46:1).

Those last three verses were written by King David. He knew he couldn't rely on himself or his subjects or his riches, nor on his status or authority. He knew his only real help was from God. David chose to F.R.O.G. So did hundreds of other people described in the Bible, as well as millions of believers who have trusted God over the centuries.

How about you? Try F.R.O.G.! God loves us. He is faithful. We can rely on him. Of course, we won't always F.R.O.G. perfectly, not on this side of heaven anyway. Still, we have to start somewhere, sometime. We may be only tadpoles at first, but with practice, we'll wind up as strong, mature F.R.O.G.s of faith.

chapter fifteen

No Fear

Have you noticed? The world and the devil want us to "Be afraid! Be very afraid!" Movies and television shows display horrific scenes, especially at Halloween. There's even a show called *Fear Factor*, the scarier the better. The Weather Channel airs programs on the "most terrifying storms of the century." Health articles imply that we're going to be sick or die if we don't do a certain exercise or take certain vitamins.

Our minds are bombarded by fear. Where our minds go, our bodies and spirits are sure to follow. We need to be on guard against these attacks. What to do?

- Don't listen!
- Don't look!
- Don't go there!

Instead, run to God and his Word for hope and peace.

Yes, I know we all have fears. It's frightening to be between jobs, to be ill or to have family problems. Of course, we all think *our* fears are the rational ones. We have good reasons for ours. Theirs, the fears we see in other people's lives, just come from a lack of faith. No, that isn't right. We should never make light of others' fears, for we haven't lived their lives. We haven't experienced their sufferings or traumas.

I'm old enough to have experienced God's love and faithfulness many times through all kinds of trials and hardship. I've surrendered many fears to him, but, I have one I give to him and take back and give to him and take back. I suffer it over and over again. I am afraid in fast, heavy traffic. It's an irrational, gut fear that we're going to be in a wreck. You may be thinking, "How childish! How stupid! How very unspiritual of her! Why doesn't she just trust God?" Believe me, I am working on it.

May I give you the background of this fear? The night before my eleventh birthday, my beautiful sixteen-year-old sister was killed in a horrible automobile accident. Five of the seven people in the car died instantly. Tragic. But people recover emotionally from much worse, and I recovered from the loss of my sister. My parents, however, kept pictures, eight by ten inch black and white glossies, of the mangled car in which my sister died. They kept them in our family photo album. I saw that wrecked car thousands of times.

Have I evoked your sympathies? Perhaps you're thinking, "Well, then, that's okay. She has a good reason to be afraid." If so, stop it. Don't sympathize with me. I need to change, to become free of that fear, with reminders from God's Word. We don't have to be fearful, no matter what our flesh, the devil, or our experiences tell us. We don't have to panic in the face of our fears. We have God's power. We can fight fear with faith.

We can push aside the pictures, the thoughts, the dread, and the ugly fear.

"God has not given us a spirit of fear (timidity or cowardice, of craven and cringing fear), but He has given us a spirit of power and of love and of a calm and well balanced mind and discipline and self-control."
—2 Timothy 1:7 AMP

Jesus says we can be peaceful instead of afraid.

"Peace I leave with you. My own peace I now give you. Not as the world gives do I give to you. Do not let your hearts be troubled, neither let them be afraid (Stop allowing yourselves to be agitated and disturbed; and do not permit yourselves to be fearful and intimidated and cowardly and unsettled.)"
—John 14:27 AMP

Those are the truths and instructions. Now, here is a scripture that tells us how to get through scary times, through uncertainties and through dark, depressing days. *"In God have I put my trust and confident reliance; I will not be afraid"* (Psalm 56:11 AMP).

"There is no fear in love, but perfect love turns fear out of doors and expels every trace of terror" (I John 4:18 AMP). That verse used to make me sad, because I thought, "I can never love perfectly, so I'll always be afraid." That isn't what it means. Who is perfect love? You've known this for a long time, "God is love." He turns away fear. The more we grow in his love by knowing it, experiencing it and giving it to others, the less fearful we will be.

When fears do try to wiggle back into our minds, the verse we need is Romans 8:15, *"You did not receive a spirit that makes you a slave again to fear, but you received the Spirit of sonship whereby we cry 'Abba Father.'"* We don't have to be slaves to our fears. We have God as our Father. We can run from the fears into his loving arms, where we will find peace and hope. I heard a Bible teacher on television say that fear is an acrostic for "False evidence appearing real." Isn't that very often the case with our fears? God does not want us to live in fear. We can all fight fear with faith.

chapter sixteen

Under His Wings

Years ago, in the Deep South, many women chose to wear a topknot. (Picture hair gathered up in a rounded ball right on the top of the head.) I read about a preacher who hated that style and decided to do something about it. One Sunday morning he preached a rousing sermon against top knots using the text "Top knot come down." At the end of the sermon, an angry woman wearing a rather pronounced topknot told the preacher that no such text as "Top not come down" could be found in the Bible. The preacher opened his King James Bible to Matthew 24:17, and pointed out the verse, "*Let him who is on the housetop not come down to take anything out of the house.*"[6]

Silly, huh? I've heard unbelievers complain that Christians can make the Bible say anything they want it to say. Maybe this story is an example of what they mean. That picky preacher was making a new rule for his church: no topknots. Imagine the arguments he must have provoked.

Isn't it sad that serious disagreements exist between denominations? Each one stresses its own rules, regulations, and traditions (some of them no more important than topknots) so strongly that we forget what Jesus really said. When asked by the religious leaders, the Pharisees,

> "*'Teacher, which is the greatest commandment in the law?' Jesus replied, 'Love the Lord your God with all your heart and with all your soul and with all your mind. This is the first and greatest commandment. And the second is like it: 'Love your neighbor as yourself.'*"
> —Matthew 22:35-39

The Pharisees had taken the commandments given to Moses by God and added so many rules and regulations that the list was almost impossible to remember, let alone obey. Of course, this made the religious leaders seem pious and powerful. Then along came Jesus, who condensed the commandments into two simple statements. Love God. Love your neighbor. In essence, Jesus robbed the leaders of their power and, as you can imagine, they hated him for that.

Jesus lived out his own commandments and did not return their hate. He loved them, and even said, when they sought to kill him, "*Jerusalem, Jerusalem, you who kill the prophets and stone those sent to you, how often I have longed to gather your children together, as a hen gathers her chicks under her wings, and you were not willing*" (Luke 13:34).

Jesus longed to take care of his people. He loved them. He longs to take care of us too. Picture God as the mother hen and us as his chicks.

- Some of us stay fairly close to him but often think about wandering off. There's a bit of something we want to explore over near the barn.
- Some of us are just pecking away in the dirt, drifting further and further away and feeling pretty proud of our independence.
- Some of us are almost out of earshot altogether.

When a dangerous storm comes up, a mother hen will "cluck" her chicks home and gather them under her wings to protect them. The ones nearby, the strutting independents, and the far off all get the same shelter, the same care. She doesn't exclude the ones who have disobeyed or wandered off.

There are times when we are like those chicks. We've been disobedient. We've fallen short so many times that we may doubt God could care about us. We may be going through such sad, confusing, or painful times that we can barely hear God's call. We just don't know where to go for help. Here's where to go: under his wings. The book of Psalms reminds us of that fact over and over:

- *"Keep me as the apple of your eye; hide me in the shadow of your wings"* (Psalm 17:8).
- *"How priceless is your unfailing love, O God! People take refuge in the shadow of your wings"* (Psalm 36:7).
- *"I will take refuge in the shadow of your wings until the disaster has passed"* (Psalm 57:1).
- *"I long to dwell in your tent forever and take refuge in the shelter of your wings"* (Psalm 61:4).

I think perhaps this one is my favorite:

- *"He will cover you with his feathers, and under his wings you will find refuge; his faithfulness will be your shield and rampart"* (Psalm 91:4).

God longs to cover each of us and shield us. We have a loving, safe place to be: under God's wings! We haven't wandered too far away to hear his voice. We just need to stop and listen.

chapter seventeen

Filtered Through Faith

I found 162 references to the word "faith" in my Bible concordance. In addition, there were 22 references to "faithfulness" and 81 to "faithful." My conclusion? God considers this an important subject.

The Greek word "pistis" means faith. It also means "to believe" in the verb form. So, to believe is to have faith.

Either we have faith that unites us with God, or we live in unbelief that separates us from him. Most of us waiver back and forth between faith and unbelief much of the time. The ninth chapter of Mark tells about a father whose son needed to be healed. After he described the boy's condition to Jesus, the father said, "If you can do anything, help us."

Doesn't that sound like us? "I'm not sure you can, but maybe you can. I'll cover my bases by at least asking. So, in case you would like to, if you are able ..."

Jesus' answer to that father is the same as what he says to us, *"All things are possible to him who believes"* (Mark 9:23 NASB).

How did that father respond? Here's what Mark 9:24 (AMP) recounts, *"At once the father of the boy gave an eager, piercing, inarticulate cry with tears and he said, 'Lord, I do believe! Help my unbelief.'"*

We can make that cry too. "I do believe, help my unbelief!" Jesus healed the man's son, and he'll help us too. But, we need to increase our faith. How do we do that? We are never, this side of heaven, going to be perfect in our faith, yet there is a way to make it grow. *"Faith comes by hearing and hearing by the word of Christ"* (Romans 10:17 NASB).

Faith comes by hearing the Word of God. The problem is, of course, that we can hear without paying attention. Remember getting called on in your high school history class? I do. Sometimes I heard the teacher's voice, but had no idea what she had asked.

We need to pay attention to God's Word, the kind of attention that comes from wanting to learn what he says. We need to hear (or read) the Bible, knowing we will benefit from what we find there. We need to let those words sink in. If we don't "pay it any mind," as we say in the South, we're sure to forget it.

I've been guilty of telling the preacher, "Good sermon this morning. It really touched me," and then letting it slip my mind. Sometime later in the afternoon, if someone asks me, "What was the sermon about today?" I have to answer, "Well, I don't remember, but it was good." If we don't meditate on God's word, it might sound good, but it won't do any real good until it reaches our hearts and produces faith.

I double dare you to hear God's Word this week. I mean get into it, read it, listen and meditate. Try starting with Hebrews, Chapter 11 (yes, the whole chapter). You'll see what people who believed God did by faith. You'll read that, "*Without faith it is impossible to please him, for whoever would draw near to God must believe that he exists and that he rewards those who seek him*" (Hebrews 11:6 ESV). Ahh, note that he rewards those who seek him, not those who seek the reward. Our drawing close to God, our belief that he is who he says he is, brings us any reward that God desires to give us.

God offers no alternative to faith as a way to approach him. We are saved by grace through faith. It isn't enough just to believe that God exists. We must believe in his goodness and seek to know him as he has been revealed to us by Christ Jesus. God asks us to go beyond doctrine, theology, or theory to a personal relationship with him through his son Jesus.

Picture for a moment an everyday coffee filter. Everything in our lives can be filtered through faith.

- We pour out our needs through faith in God. Out comes God's provision, exactly what we need, even if we don't realize it.

- We pour our doubts through our faith. Out comes confidence in God, that blessed assurance!
- We pour our fears and worries through faith in God. Out comes peace, peace that the world cannot understand.
- We pour our guilt and shame through faith, and out comes our righteousness through God's forgiveness.
- We pour our weakness through faith in God, and out comes his strength, that strength that assures us, "I can do all things through Christ."

We can face anything, any situation. How? With faith in God. Why? Because God loves us and wants what is best for us. He knows what is best for us and has the power to bring it about. With him all things are possible. And that's why we can filter everything in our lives through our faith in God.

chapter eighteen

Yellow Ribbons

Many of us tie yellow ribbons around trees or mailboxes, or put yellow ribbon decals on our cars, as reminders to support and pray for our military personnel around the world. They deserve our daily prayers. Yellow ribbons also stand for forgiveness. Do you remember the singer Tony Orlando? One of his hits was "Tie a Yellow Ribbon 'Round the Old Oak Tree." It hit number one on the music charts in April 1973. (Perhaps you were just a baby at the time. Maybe you weren't even born yet. In that case, consider this a history lesson.) The song was based on an American folk tale that went something like this.

A man who had given his wife plenty of grief finally left her. Eventually, he was arrested and sent to prison for writing bad checks. While serving his three-year sentence, he realized what a scoundrel he had been. He was sorry for all the mistakes he had made and for the hurt he had caused his family.

When he was about to be released from prison, he wrote a letter to his wife and asked her to forgive him. He also said he would understand if she never wanted to see him again. He explained that he would be taking a particular bus that would go through their hometown. If she wanted him to get off the bus and come home, she was to tie a yellow ribbon around the oak tree in the city square.

Imagine the man's anxiety as the bus got closer and closer. He was so nervous that he couldn't bring himself to look. He asked the bus driver to be on the lookout in order to tell him what he saw. When the town came into view, there were yellow ribbons on every branch.[7] He was forgiven. What a wonderful feeling!

We can all have that feeling, that joy, that release from sin and regret, because God forgives us. We can come home to him. No matter what we've done, God says it's forgivable. When we believe in him and ask him to forgive us, he does. The greatest of all freedoms is the forgiveness of sin.

- In Matthew 9:2, when Jesus said to the paralyzed man, "*Take heart, son; your sins are forgiven,*" that was his most important healing right there. But then Jesus healed the man physically to show that he had the authority to forgive sin.
- In Matthew 26:28, as he passed out the wine during the last supper, Jesus said, "*This is my blood of the new covenant, which is poured out for many for the forgiveness of sins.*" What a price He paid for us! We can be forgiven because Christ paid the debt for our sin.
- In Luke 24:47, when Christ appeared to his disciples after his resurrection, he reminded them that repentance and forgiveness were to be preached in his name.
- Peter said of Christ in Acts 10:43, "*All the prophets testify about him that everyone who believes in him receives forgiveness of sins through his name.*"

Everyone who believes! This is not an exclusive promise, not just for certain people. Everyone! We may be tempted to think, "Yeah, right. Sure it is. But nobody knows how bad I am, how wicked my heart is, what evil thoughts I have, and what terrible things I do. No way can I be forgiven."

My answer is a wholehearted, "Yes, way." We are promised in 1 John that if we confess our sins, admitting them to God, he will forgive us and make us clean again. Then, having been forgiven ourselves, we are to forgive others. Jesus told us that, "*if you forgive other people when they sin against you, your heavenly Father will also forgive you. But if you do not forgive others their sins, your Father will not forgive your sins*" (Matthew 6:14-15). Paul reiterated that by telling members of the early church to forgive one another as the Lord forgave them.

Forgiveness isn't always easy. Sometimes, we think, "I can't do that. They don't deserve forgiveness. I don't feel like forgiving them. What they did was too horrible." The truth is, if God tells us in his Word to forgive, then we can forgive. He never tells us to do something without giving us the power to do it. Forgiving isn't a feeling, it's a choice.

This very day, if there's someone we haven't forgiven, it's time to get alone with God and do it. Our prayer may sound something like this, "God, I don't feel like I want to do this, but as an act of my will, by choice, I obey you. I choose to forgive this person. You can change my feelings. I will no longer rehearse the grievances and bitterness I have. I forgive them as you have forgiven me. Help me to be kind, tender hearted, and forgiving, as you have forgiven me."

The next step? We must leave it with God. We must not take it back. When those old feelings rise up, we have to say, "No Way! I have forgiven that person as I have been forgiven." And when can we stop forgiving others? Never. Because God never stops forgiving us. Jesus has yellow ribbons tied around everything. He tells us, "All is forgiven. I'm waiting for you with open arms."

chapter nineteen

Eye Level

I like stories about wishes granted by some magical power. How many movies have followed that Cinderella theme? My children loved the tale of three wishes given to the foolish husband and wife. The husband wished for a sausage. His infuriated wife wished it attached to his nose. The final wish had to be used to get the sausage off his nose, and so they ended up with nothing. The moral of the story: be careful what you wish for. The choices we make are important, even if they're wishes bestowed by a genie.

God is not a magic genie to be used as our servant. Our relationship with him is just the opposite. We are his servants. I want us to consider a question that Jesus asked someone, and I'd like to suggest that he still asks the same question of us. We find that question in Mark 10:46-52:

"Then they came to Jericho. As Jesus and his disciples, together with a large crowd, were leaving the city, a blind man, Bartimaeus (which means "son of Timaeus"), was sitting by the roadside begging. When he heard that it was Jesus of Nazareth, he began to shout, 'Jesus, Son of David, have mercy on me!'

Many rebuked him and told him to be quiet, but he shouted all the more, 'Son of David, have mercy on me!'

Jesus stopped and said, 'Call him.'

So they called to the blind man, 'Cheer up! On your feet! He's calling you.' Throwing his cloak aside, he jumped to his feet and came to Jesus.

'What do you want me to do for you?' Jesus asked him.
The blind man said, 'Rabbi, I want to see.'
'Go,' said Jesus, 'your faith has healed you.' Immediately he re-
ceived his sight and followed Jesus along the road."

This account holds so many good lessons for us, but I want to concentrate on the question, "What do you want me to do for you?" Doesn't that seem strange? Jesus knew he was blind. What other answer could Jesus have expected? Hold that thought as I tell you another story.

This story was shared with me some years ago by an acquaintance whose name I have changed to John. John was out of work for a long time. He and his family had moved in with his father. Then his father was laid off. John went through some hard, discouraging, and scary times.

One day, John took his little daughter Sarah for a walk. Having time to do that was one benefit of being unemployed. He decided to buy her a treat. This was unusual for two reasons. One, John and his wife were very strict about junk food. Two, they seldom spent money on treats. John and Sarah walked to a local convenience store for the big event, the splurge. You know how candy is displayed in those stores: high racks, with the cheap candy on the bottom, and the better stuff up higher at eye level. Sarah, being much smaller than her very tall father, began to look with great delight at the brightly colored, cartoonishly wrapped, inexpensive candy. That candy was so cheap, it didn't even qualify as a splurge.

John said, "No, Sarah, look up here. There's the really good stuff. You can choose anything, not just what's down there." But she was sure of what she wanted, and picked some bright red balls of candy. Loving father that he is, John said, "Sarah, those are sour balls, very sour. I know you, and you won't like them. Look, here's a Snickers, or a Nestlé Crunch bar. But Sarah would have nothing to do with that. She saw only what was right in front of her, at her own eye level, and she ended up with something cheap. It wasn't the best she could have had, and was nowhere near what her father wanted to give her. He told me he was disappointed that his desire to give Sarah something special, something big, went unfulfilled.

59

John went on to describe how God used the experience to reveal to him that he, John, often fell into the same situation in his relationship with his heavenly Father that Sarah had with him that day. He was making some poor choices, because he could see the situation only at his eye level, while his heavenly Father saw the whole picture. Our Father sees what's best for us better than we can. We are limited by our own "short sightedness." We can't see the top shelf, so we often choose a lollipop over a king size Snickers bar.

"*I have come that they may have life, and have it to the full*" (John 10:10). Our Father knows what we will like and what will fulfill us, because he created us. He knows what will make us happy better than we know ourselves. We might choose red sourballs because they look good, instead of letting God give us the desires he has created in our hearts. He puts his desires there. Note our part in this scripture. "*Trust in the Lord and do good; dwell in the land and enjoy safe pasture. Take delight in the Lord, and he will give you the desires of your heart*" (Psalm 37:3-4).

Do we take away God's joy in giving to us because we want to do it ourselves, our own way? Sarah wanted her own way and got it. We aren't perfect, and we probably seldom touch the depth of this next verse. But it is what we aim for. "*Trust in the Lord with all your heart; do not depend on your own understanding. Seek His will in all you do, and he will show you which path to take*" Proverbs 3:5-6 (NLT).

What if, today, Jesus asked us the question, "What do you want me to do for you?" We're human. We'd say we wanted a job, healing, a house, a car, the return of a wayward child, or maybe even three magic wishes. Wait. Stop. Think. Jesus knows our needs. We can tell him what we think we need, but then we ought to tell him, "Whatever you think is best. Your will be done." We can trust his love, rely on his wisdom, and believe in his power.

If we want God's best, we must let him choose.

chapter twenty

The Fretnotters' Club

Are you a worrywart? Do you fret about everything? Worrying is something most of us do even if we don't want to do it. Many of us live our lives saying of the past, "If only" and of the future, "What if?" Barbara Johnson once wrote that, "Worry is wasting today's time to clutter up tomorrow's opportunities with yesterday's troubles."[8]

I think people can become addicted to worry. If they don't have something to worry about, they'll worry about not having anything to worry about. Shakespeare wrote in his play *Julius Caesar*, "A coward dies a thousand times before his death." He dies over and over again, because he worries about it, frets over it, and imagines it. We're not meant to go through life like that. There's a better way.

Today I'm establishing a new club and challenging you to join. I'm hoping it will become an international sensation. It's based on Psalm 37:1, *"Do not fret because of those who are evil."* The club is appropriately named "The Fretnotters." In Australia, "No worries, mate!" is a common expression. Perhaps that could become our motto.

There's no monetary investment required to join this club, but there are a few rules. (You knew that was coming.) I'll summarize them, but the complete list of rules and bylaws is found in Psalm 37. Feel free to read the entire chapter before you join. Be advised that the chapter doesn't just tell us to stop fretting. It also tells us how to stop that nasty habit, and what will happen when we do.

Rules for Fretnotters:

- Rule One: "*Trust in the Lord (lean on Him; rely on Him) and do good*" (Psalm 37:3 AMP). Benefit: We will dwell safely in the land and enjoy God's faithfulness.
- Rule Two: "*Take delight in the Lord*" (Psalm 37:4). Be glad he is your Lord. Enjoy His commands. Benefit: He will cause us to want his will for our lives, and then he will fulfill that desire.
- Rule Three: "*Commit your ways to the Lord. Roll over and rest each care of your load on Him and be confident in him*" (Psalm 37:5 AMP). Benefit: He will make our righteousness obvious and highlight the justice of our cause.
- Rule Four: "*Be still and rest in the Lord; wait for Him and patiently lean yourself upon him*" (Psalm 37:7 AMP). Isn't that a cry of our hearts? Most of us long to just stop and relax for a while. It's time to cease trying to make things happen long enough to listen to God. Benefit: Diminished worry.
- Rule Five: "*Refrain from anger. Turn from wrath. Don't envy*" (Psalm 37:8-9 author's paraphrase.) Benefit: A decrease in doing and saying wrong things in our lives.

Now about that last rule, sometimes we think, "Well thank God, I'm not an angry person. There's no wrath in me." Ahh, but do we hate anyone? Do we experience road rage? Can we read the newspaper without having our blood pressure rise? How many times do we raise our voices unnecessarily to our loved ones or grit our teeth to keep from yelling? Maybe we all have a little more anger in us than we like to admit.

God describes the fate of the wicked in verses 12-22 of our club's bylaws (Psalm 37). Clearly, as Fretnotters, we do not expect to suffer their fate, but we should always take God's warnings seriously.

Finally, in verses 23-40, God lovingly details even more of the benefits he bestows on those who trust and obey him, on Fretnotters. It's a great list. He will delight in us, make our steps firm, and direct our paths. When we stumble, we won't fall, because he'll hold us up. (This is a very important promise, because we will stumble as we attempt to obey these club rules.) God says he won't forsake us, and he'll protect us. Instead of requiring a pledge from us, God makes one to us in the last two verses of Psalm 37. I've changed pronouns, but not the meaning. Here's God's pledge to Fretnotters. Imagine him saying this to you.

> *"The salvation of the godly comes from me, your Lord. I am your stronghold in times of trouble. I help you and I deliver you and save you, because you take refuge in me."*

Because we are in his care, we need not worry or fret, ever. Go on – enjoy God. Become a full time member of the Fretnotters' Club.

chapter twenty-one

Never Forgotten

W e all have times when we forget things. At my age, we call them "senior moments." Sometimes I'll see an old friend out in public and just can't remember the name that goes with the familiar face. Personally, I'd like to say that I have a photographic memory. The thing is, most of the time I forget to take the lens cap off. As for my husband Bert, poor thing, sometimes he forgets my birthday, our anniversary, and who's boss.

I wonder if we sometimes think God has forgotten us. The truth is that we often forget him. Israel, his covenant people, forgot him over and over. They'd disobey him and worship idols. Then, when they were invaded by an enemy country or suffered famine or some other disaster, they would think about God once again and call out to him, "Remember us! Save us! Care for us with your kindness and mercy." God would help them. Then, when the danger passed, they would forget God again. Such a vicious cycle! Doesn't that sound a little like us?

Anytime we feel far away from God, we're the ones who have moved, not God. Maybe we haven't gone years without thinking of God, but have we gone months without acknowledging him, or weeks without praying to him? Have we missed days without praising or thanking him? Jeremiah 3:21 describes the problem by saying, "*A cry is heard…because they have perverted their ways and have forgotten the Lord their God.*" One version says, "They have wandered far away from his ways."

We're prone to wander. This has always been true of us humans. Robert Robinson wrote these words in 1758. Maybe you remember them from an old hymn. "Prone to wander, Lord I feel it, prone to leave the God I love."[9] Why would we do that? I don't know why, yet some of us have. We want to cry out to him for help. That's a good thing! God has lovingly provided words we can use as we cry out to him for help. These verses are from Psalm 25:6-7(NLT). *"Remember, O Lord, your compassion and unfailing love, which you have shown from long ages past. Do not remember the rebellious sins of my youth* (I add "and my old age" here). *Remember me in the light of your unfailing love, for you are merciful, O Lord."* What comes after our cry for help? Confession of sin and asking him for forgiveness. He promises to forgive us, and he does.

We forget God, don't we? But rest assured he does not forget us. Not ever. When the Israelites declared that the Lord had forgotten them, this is how he answered them.

"Never! Can a mother forget her nursing child? Can she feel no love for a child she has borne? But, even if that were possible, I would not forget you. See, I have written your name on the palms of my hand."
—Isaiah 49:15-16 NLT

One version of the Bible says the name is "tattooed." That means that nothing is going to wash it away.

The Bible is full of affirmations of God's love for us. The greatest, of course, is that Jesus died for our sins. He gave his life for us so that we may live in his kingdom while we're on earth and then have everlasting life in heaven. Many of us, when our children were young, would ask them, "How much do you love me?" We taught them to open their arms wide and say, "I love you this much." God opened his arms wide on the cross saying, "I love you this much." Let's look carefully in our minds at that picture. Do we see our names on his hands? If we've come to trust Christ and accepted him as Lord and Savior, our names are there, tattooed forever. He doesn't forget us, even when we ignore him.

What does a child do when someone who loves him opens his arms wide and says, "Come on"? The child runs to that person and feels the love, security, and comfort offered by those arms as they draw him close. I intend to do some running into God's arms today, for I am prone to wander from him and to forget so easily all he has done. Won't you run there with me?

Let's remember him. He never forgets us. He loves us this much! And he says, "Come on."

chapter twenty-two

Amazingly Able

Matthew chapter 9 recounts a story of two blind men who called out to Jesus, saying, "Have mercy on us, Son of David." (They had heard that Jesus could heal.)

Jesus asked them an important question, "Do you believe I'm able to do this?"

Doesn't Jesus ask us the same thing when we come to him with our requests? We pray, "Lord, help me. I need _____. (You fill in the blank.)" Can God really answer our prayers? Do we believe that he is able? Sometimes we give lip service to our belief that God is all powerful, but our hearts are not convinced. God's Word is completely clear and convincing. He tells us over and over again that he is fully able to meet every one of our needs.

Bill Hybels did a wonderful job of recounting God's power in a book entitled *Too Busy Not to Pray.*[10] He reminded his readers of the importance of asking God to insert his power and presence into our lives. You and I have the same Bible that Pastor Hybels has, and it tells us that God has:

- parted the seas.
- caused water to gush from a rock.
- provided food from heaven.
- prolonged daylight.
- calmed a storm.
- multiplied fish and bread.

Clearly nature must obey the will God, but can he get us out of troubling circumstances? Yes, he can. He broke Peter out of jail in the middle of the night, even though that man of God was chained between two guards and watched by at least a dozen more. Peter was astonished by the angel who came to get him and wondered if he was dreaming. When the angel left him in the street, though, Peter hightailed it to a home where believers were gathered. When he knocked on the door, a young girl saw him. She squealed with joy, slammed the door shut in Peter's face, and ran to tell the others. "You're crazy!" they told her. (They were just as slow to believe that God can miraculously change circumstances as we are.) They thought perhaps Peter had been killed and his angel was at the door. The knocking continued. When they finally opened the door, they were amazed by God's power. I haven't been in more trouble than that, have you? I think God can handle whatever we might face. But what about our own sinful, messed up selves?

That same man, Peter, who could fall asleep between two guards as he awaited almost certain death, had been a man full of fear just years earlier. Exactly as Jesus predicted, he denied that he knew our Lord. In fact, he denied him three times, afraid that he too would be arrested. Jesus changed Peter from a chicken to a lion. He can change us too. We serve the same Lord who calmed the storms, rescued Peter, and then turned him into a fearless evangelist. He tells us that he is the same yesterday, today and forever. (Check out Hebrews 13:8.)

God is powerful. God is able. We need to remind ourselves of that over and over, to really get it into our hearts. When we pray, we need to do as the two blind men before Christ did and say, "Yes, Lord, you are able to do all things."

Here are just a few of the things God's word reminds us that God does:

- He keeps his word and does what he promises (Romans 4:21).
- He provides all we need so that we can share with others (2 Corinthians 9:8).
- He gives us the strength to do his work (1 Timothy 1:12).

And I love this one, "*God is able [to carry out His purpose and] to do super abundantly, far over and above, all that we dare to ask or think [infinitely beyond our highest prayers, thoughts, hopes or dreams]*" (Ephesians 3:20 AMP).

Oh how we thrive when we know deep in our hearts that we serve an awesome and powerful God! We want to own that fact, to bank on it, and to live within its security. We want to let God demonstrate his power and ability in our lives. And we can, because God says we can do all things through Christ.

chapter twenty-three

Our Gardener

Way back when I was teaching high school English, there was a popular poster that some of us put up in our classrooms. It was a picture of a flower growing out of a tiny crack in a mass of rocks. The caption read, "Bloom where you're planted." That's a good idea, maybe even a little inspirational, but how typical of a teacher to tell you to do something without giving you so much as a clue as to how to do it!

So, how do we bloom in God's garden? God is a gardener who plants with a purpose. He has created us to bring him glory. That's the reason for our existence. Since he planted us for that purpose, I believe he's got a whole lot of cultivating to do so that we can glorify him. As the very best gardener, God puts us in the very best soil. He sets our roots in his love. And oh what love! In Ephesians 3:17-19, Paul writes: "*I pray that you, being rooted and established in love, may have power, together with all the Lord's holy people, to grasp how wide and long and high and deep is the love of Christ, and to know this love that surpasses knowledge.*" Rooted in love. God's love is a good place to be set deep.

Once we're planted, God takes care of us so that we can grow. He waters us. I know you've seen plants and flowers all curled up and about to die because of drought conditions. How do they look after a good rain? It's almost as if they are brought back from the dead, all plumped up and beautiful once again. We get all droopy and dried up if we don't read God's Word. If you feel as if you're going through a dry period, Isaiah 58:11 (NLT) provides this encouragement, "*The Lord will guide you continually, giving you water when you are dry and restoring your strength. You will be like a well-watered garden, like an ever-flowing spring."* Get in there. Read his Word. Get watered.

God also feeds his garden. We are fed by his Word as well as watered by it. I found a verse about being fed that I love. It's from the *Amplified Version* and does not appear exactly the same way in any other version that I studied. It says, *"Trust (lean on, rely on, and be confident) in the Lord and do good; so shall you dwell in the land and feed surely on his faithfulness, and truly you shall be fed"* (Psalm 37:3 AMP). I think faithfulness must be God's Weed & Feed product. As we feed on his faithfulness, we begin to see that we can trust him more and more. That trust begins to kill the weeds of fear and doubt and worry. Do you need an extra serving? I know I do. Good news! The Bible says God gives us our food just as we need it. When we look to him, he gives it to us at the proper time. (See Psalm 145:15.)

God, our gardener, has another job that we don't like to talk about very much. Plants must be pruned to keep them healthy. Jesus discussed pruning with his disciples in the first few verses of John, Chapter 15. He said God cuts off branches that bear no fruit, trimming and cleaning the ones that do bear fruit to make them even more fruitful. Then he told his disciples they were already cleaned and pruned because of the words he had spoken to them. We are pruned by the teachings of Jesus if we heed his words.

Pruning involves cutting away anything that is unnecessary or a hindrance to fruitfulness. God's pruning makes us more productive in his kingdom. It may be painful to us, and we may not agree with God about what is unnecessary, about what needs to go. Of course, we know in our spirits that God knows best. Hard as it is, we need to say, "Cut away, Lord."

God also mulches us. Mulch is used around plants to keep water from evaporating. It also keep the roots warm. He covers our roots all around with love to protect us. He mulches us to keep us from growing cold in our love for him or dry in our faith. The brand of mulch he uses is called Love and Forgiveness, and it only comes in extra-large containers.

In winter weather, we often see tarps or old sheets and tablecloths thrown over plants to protect them. Sometimes plants are even moved indoors to keep them away from the chill. God has a way to protect us in cold, hard, and difficult times. He uses his mighty power to shield us. Isn't it great to be in the garden of a powerful owner? Read Psalm 121 sometime soon. It will confirm God's care and protection of you.

While God tends to us, what can we do?

- Let's get in his presence. Pray.
- Let's get in his Word. Read and obey.
- Let's submit to his pruning without complaint.

In the hands of the master gardener we can be sure we'll grow just right. We'll flower. We'll be fruitful. We'll fulfill our purpose, to glorify him. That's the way we'll show God's love and goodness to the world around us.

chapter twenty-four

Lifesavers

A man died and met St. Peter at the pearly gates. Peter said to the man, "Here's how it works. You need to have 100 points to get into heaven. Tell me about all the good things you've done. They're all worth a certain number of points. If your total is 100 or more, you can come in."

"Well," said the man. "I was happily married to the same woman for 52 years. I never looked at another woman. I was attentive and loved her dearly."

"That's great," said St. Peter. "That'll be two points."

"Hmmm," the man thought aloud, "This is going to be harder than I expected. Well, I attended church regularly, volunteered my time, and tithed faithfully."

"Wonderful! That's worth another point."

"One point!" the man exclaimed. "Okay, okay. I was involved with a prison ministry for twenty-five years. I went into the prison every month and shared Jesus with them."

"Wow!" said St. Peter. "That's another two points!"

"Only two points!" said the discouraged soul. "At this rate, I'll only get into this place by the grace of God."

"Bingo!" cried St. Peter. "That's one hundred points! Come on in."[11]

God's grace—that's our way into eternal life and our way to live here on earth, day in and day out. Grace is God's unearned, undeserved favor to man.

Remember those rolls of candy called Lifesavers? Well, grace is, quite literally, our lifesaver. We're saved for eternity by God's grace, and we're sustained here on earth every day by his grace.

"God is so rich in mercy, and he loved us so much, that even though we were dead because of our sins, he gave us life when he raised Christ from the dead. (It is only by God's grace that you have been saved!) For he raised us from the dead along with Christ and seated us with him in the heavenly realms because we are united with Christ Jesus. So God can point to us in all future ages as examples of the incredible wealth of his grace and kindness toward us, as shown in all he has done for us who are united with Christ Jesus. God saved you by his grace when you believed. And you can't take credit for this; it is a gift from God. Salvation is not a reward for the good things we have done, so none of us can boast about it."

—Ephesians 2:4-9 NLT

Indulge me for a minute while I make sure you've absorbed the truth in those verses. Here's a little pop quiz about grace. I'll ask the questions. And if you've understood the passage, your answers will be, in this order, "no, no, never, noooo, not a chance, and no!" (If you're reading this in public, I hope you will answer under your breath.)

- Can you buy it?
- Can you inherit it from your mom and dad?
- Can you get it because you're talented or smart?
- Can you do enough good works, get enough gold stars, to erase the black marks on your record of life?
- Can you earn it?
- When you get it, can you brag about it?

We've settled the fact that grace is God's gift and our eternal lifesaver, but what about right now? How do we live "by grace" until we die and begin our eternal life? Jesus said that once we are believers we have already passed from death into life. So, as believers in Christ, we're already able to rely on God's grace every day. His power far exceeds our own resources. In fact, lucky for us, his power shows up best in weak people who submit themselves to him.

Sometimes truth and feelings collide, but truth is truth and feelings are feelings. Never do the second change the first. We may say, "I don't feel that God loves me or cares for me." That doesn't change the truth that he does indeed love you and care for you. Truth never ceases to exist just because we choose to ignore it. We may ignore the fact that we're saved by God's grace. That doesn't change the truth of it.

Now you have the facts about God's grace. It's amazing. That's the word John Newton used to describe grace in the hymn he wrote, *Amazing Grace*.

Maybe you've seen the documentary made by Bill Moyers on the hymn *Amazing Grace*. One of the scenes shows Wembley Stadium in London, where several bands gathered for a rock festival. The concert lasted for twelve hours, and you can imagine the mood of the crowd by the end of that time, many of them high on alcohol and drugs. The festival concluded with a song by an opera singer named Jessye Norman. She chose "Amazing Grace." Without any accompaniment, she began to sing slowly:

Amazing Grace! How sweet the sound,
That saved a wretch like me!
I once was lost, but now I'm found;
Was blind, but now I see.[12]

By the time she reached the last verse, a strange power had descended upon the stadium. All was quiet. We are all amazed by grace. We thirst for it. And Christ offers it to us, both now and for eternity.

chapter twenty-five

Precious Pearls

D o you collect anything? My pastor collects walking sticks and canes. My daughter collects nativity sets. My grandson used to collect keychains. And my good friend Joan collects jewelry.

Joan and I have known each other for over forty years. She loves jewelry the way I love chocolate. For as long as I can remember, if we were out shopping together, she'd stop at jewelry stores to look for a particular stone she wanted for her collection. I was always drooling in front of the Godiva store. Meanwhile, she would say, "I'm trying to find a light blue sapphire, or a purple one. I need a citrine that's very yellow. You know the mines where they find them are almost depleted." She really knows her stones. I know my chocolate. I can tell a Hershey Kiss from a Dove Bar any day.

Joan had specific plans for her treasure. Some of the pieces were so valuable that she had fake copies made to look like them. She wore the fakes and left the real ones in the safe. (This does not work with chocolate. Hidden chocolate tends to melt. Fake chocolate, also known as carob, is Yuk!) One day, about twenty years ago, she finally showed her whole treasure collection to me. It took more than an hour just to look at it—beautiful rings and bracelets and even some loose stones not yet set.

What a treasure! I think some of her other friends and I were just a bit envious. Whenever Joan tried to complain that something was too expensive, we would respond by saying, "Well, you know, you could always sell some of your jewelry." Now, that was just mean. If I had complained about being overweight, she could have said, "Well, you could always stop eating chocolate." I wouldn't have liked that.

We all have something we treasure. Perhaps that's why Jesus told two parables about treasure. They're recorded in the book of Matthew, Chapter 13. Jesus used parables, simple stories of everyday life, to teach his followers spiritual truths. So, when we read a parable, we ought to ask ourselves, "What are the spiritual lessons we can learn from this story?" With that in mind, take a look at Matthew 13:44. *"The kingdom of God is like a treasure hidden in a field. When a man found it, he hid it again and then in joy went and sold all he had and bought the field."* The interpretation I offer you today may not be the one you've always accepted, and it isn't my own. It's from a book called *Extravagant Love* by a wonderful Bible scholar named Derek Prince.[13]

Dr. Prince suggested we look at the parable this way.

- The man in the parable is Jesus.
- The field represents the world.
- The treasure stands for God's people in the world.

The man found the treasure and bought the whole field. Did he want the whole field? No, but he realized in order to get the treasure, he had to buy the whole field. It cost him all he had, but he gladly paid the high price, because he knew the value of the treasure contained in the field.

Consider John 3:16 in light of the parable. *"For God so loved the world that he gave his one and only son, Jesus, that whoever believes in him shall not perish, but shall have eternal life."* The "whoevers," the people who believe in him, are the treasure in the field, the people Jesus died to save. He paid for the whole world in order to redeem the "whoevers." He bought the whole field for his treasure, his redeemed people.

God is not willing that anyone be lost. The door is open. He died for the whole world. He wants everyone to be a believer. Whosoever will may come. Jesus gave his all for the treasure, for those who believe in him.

Now, let's look at the second parable about a valuable treasure. Matthew 13:45-46. Jesus said, *"Again, the kingdom of heaven is like a merchant looking for fine pearls. When he found one of great value, he went and sold everything he had and bought it."*

Perhaps in this parable the merchant is also Jesus. Note that he wasn't just meandering around window shopping. He knew what he was seeking. When he found the one pearl, he knew he had found something of great value, something worth a sky high purchase price. The cost for the field and the pearl were the same, all he had.

In the first parable, Jesus was talking about a treasure collection, the believers as a group. In the second, he was talking about one single pearl, one believer. Picture Jesus holding one single pearl in his hand. Imagine him saying, "I gave my all, my very life, just for you." Jesus loves each of us that much. Each of us can say, "If I had been the only one on earth that needed to be redeemed, Jesus would have died just for me."

Do you struggle with a sense of shame or worthlessness? Do you wonder whether or not God really wants you, loves you, or cares about you? Stop now. Let this parable convince you that you are a pearl, greatly loved by Christ.

The next time you see a pearl, or any sort of gem for that matter, let it remind you that you are precious, of great worth. Christ proved it. He gave his all for you.

chapter twenty-six

Sweeter than Honey

When does a bee say, "Zzub, zzub"? When he's flying backward. Why does a bee hum? Because he doesn't know the words.

Let me tell you a bit about bees. A honeybee has two stomachs, a regular one and one that's just for the nectar he sucks from flowers. A bee may have to visit anywhere from 100 to 1500 flowers to fill that stomach. When it's full, the bee goes back to the hive and passes the nectar to other worker bees that chew the substance for about thirty minutes, mixing enzymes in with the nectar. Then those bees spread the mixture into honeycombs where water evaporates, making a thicker syrup.

In order to speed up the evaporation process, bees fan the honeycomb with their wings. Then they seal the comb cells with wax. The honey is stored there until it's eaten. In one year, a colony of bees eats between 120 and 200 pounds of honey. It takes the nectar from about 2,000,000 flowers to make just one pound of honey. To produce that one pound of honey, bees may need to travel a distance equal to twice the circumference of the earth.

It's no wonder honey has been a treasured substance throughout history.

- In the Old Testament, when Jacob wanted to send a valuable gift to Egypt, he included honey.
- God supernaturally supplied food to the Israelites when they were wandering in the wilderness. It was called manna and is described as tasting like wafers with honey.

- In 1 Kings 14:3, a package assembled to bribe the prophet Ahijah contained bread, cakes, and a jar of honey.

In many places in the Bible, the words of God are equated with honey.

"The law of the Lord is perfect, refreshing the soul. The statutes of the Lord are trustworthy, making wise the simple. The precepts of the Lord are right, giving joy to the heart. The commands of the Lord are radiant, giving light to the eyes. The fear of the Lord is pure, enduring forever. The decrees of the Lord are firm, and all of them are righteous. They are more precious than gold, than much pure gold; they are sweeter than honey, than honey from the honeycomb."

—Psalm 19:7-10

"How sweet are your words to my taste, sweeter than honey to my mouth."

—Psalm 119:103

"Eat honey, my son, for it is good; honey from the comb is sweet to your taste. Know also that wisdom is like honey for you: If you find it, there is a future hope for you, and your hope will not be cut off."

—Proverbs 24:13-14

God's Word is wisdom, and it's as sweet as honey to our souls. In his Word we find our eternal hope. And so we need to "eat" God's Word, to read and devour and search and study it. We know that, but we often take the Bible for granted. We can read it any time we want to. It's readily available. Some of us probably have several copies of the Bible.

God's Word is like honey, once so valued and hard to come by. When honey was the only source of sweetness, it was searched for and treasured. We no longer think of honey in that way. It's available all of the time. We can walk into most grocery stores and get a one pound jug, the amount of honey that requires bees to travel the equivalent of two times around the earth. We don't give that a thought. We just go in and get it for a few dollars. We don't really treasure honey any more.

Maybe because we can just walk over to the table and pick up a Bible any old time, we no longer think of it as precious, full of sweet tasting wisdom. What if, suddenly, there were no Bibles? What if we had to depend upon each other for memorized verses and stories? What if it were against the law to have a Bible or to speak the scriptures out loud? What if we had to use codes and symbols to remind each other of God's love, of his promises? Then would we realize how precious God's words are? That's something to think about.

I hope every time we eat honey, or anything sweet, our thought will be "Yum, that's good! But the Word of God is even better." Maybe this would make a good diet. Instead of eating the "sweets" of the world, we could "eat" the sweet Word of God. I bet we could lose a lot of weight with that plan and bulk up our spirits at the same time.

Get a Bible. Read it. Taste and see that the Lord is good! And include a bit of sweetness in every day.

chapter twenty-seven

Whose World is it Anyway?

T he song "He's Got the Whole World in His Hands" was popular when my children were young. I believed it then, and I believe it now. At times, though, it feels to me as if God doesn't really have "the whole world in his hands." I get frustrated by the direction the world seems to be taking.

Nearly every day something happens that causes us to shake our heads and wonder, "How did the world get so crazy?" We can get pretty depressed about our planet earth. But I've got good news! The world does indeed belong to God, because he created it. He didn't create the mess it's in now. Sin has done that, through man. But, let me encourage you with these verses.

> *"Oh God, the heavens are yours and the earth is yours; everything in the world is yours – you created it all."*
>
> —Psalm 89:11 NLT

> *"The earth is the Lord's and everything in it. The world and all its people belong to him."*
>
> —Psalm 24:1 NLT

> *"This is what the Lord says: Heaven is my throne and the earth is my footstool. Could you build me a temple as good as that? Could you build me such a resting place? My hands have made both heaven and earth; they and everything in them are mine."*
>
> —Isaiah 66:1-2 NLT

We can dwell on the negative aspects of our world, or we can proclaim God's ownership. We begin by being certain that God is the owner of our own worlds, of our lives and of our circumstances. Then we must place our personal world at his throne and let him be the King.

A young boy once told his dad, "I know what the Bible stands for." The father answered, "That's a lot to know. What does it stand for?" The boy replied, "BIBLE – Basic Instructions Before Leaving Earth."

One way to place our world in his hands is to use those instructions to declare what God's Word says. We can say with authority and conviction whatever he says, because his Word is always right and true. Here's a great passage. If these verses don't make us happy, don't lift our spirits, I don't know what will. This chapter describes how the earth and everything on the earth, including us, should respond to the fact that God is the creator and keeper of the world.

> *"Let the whole earth sing to the Lord! Each day proclaim the good news that he saves. Publish his glorious deeds among the nations. Tell everyone about the amazing things he does. Worship the Lord in all his holy splendor. Let all the earth tremble before him. The world is firmly established and cannot be shaken. Let the heavens be glad, and let the earth rejoice! Tell all the nations that the Lord is king. Let the sea and everything in it shout his praise! Let the fields and their crops burst forth with joy! Let the trees of the forest rustle with praise before the Lord! For he is coming to judge the earth. Give thanks to the LORD, for he is good!"*
>
> —1 Chronicles 16 NLT, abridged

Ah, yes! Isn't that great? That's the response we should have to God. And what is God's response to the world? You may already know John 3:16-17; but here it is from *The Amplified Version*. I hope you'll read it several times this week.

> *"For God so loved and dearly prized the world that He even gave up His only begotten son, so that whoever believes in, trusts in, clings to, and relies on Him shall not perish, come to destruction or be lost, but shall have everlasting life. For God did not send the Son into the world in order to*

judge, reject, condemn or pass sentence on the world, but that the world might find salvation and be made safe and sound through Him."

Knowing how dearly God loves us, let's not exclude him. Let's embrace his love, his mercy, his forgiveness, and his grace. If you've never done that, you can do it today. I did it one Monday morning many years ago after all my young children were off at school. Alone in the house at the foot of my bed, I became one of the "whosoever believes" people talked about in John 3:16. It has made all the difference. Let's put him at the center of our worlds. Let God be in charge and in control. Try it. You'll love it.

Some of you may know the old hymn "This Is My Father's World," written by Maltbie D. Babcock in 1901. The last verse reads:

This is my Father's world, O let me ne'er forget
That though the wrong seems oft so strong,
God is the ruler yet.
This is my Father's world; why should my heart be sad?
The Lord is King; let the heavens ring!
God reigns; let the earth be glad.

I pray that this truth will make us glad this week, and that we'll remember to keep our world in his hands.

chapter twenty-eight

No Bones About It

Wˣe talk about our bones in all sorts of unusual ways. Perhaps you've heard the expression, "Man! I am bone tired today." That means you're really exhausted. Here are three more bony phrases:

- "I can feel it in my bones." That could mean something good is going to happen, or something bad, or maybe just that the weather is changing.
- "I've got a bone to pick with you." Uh, oh. That usually starts an argument.
- "I'll make no bones about it," means we are going to tell the truth (or that a politician wants us to believe something is the truth).

David, the king and psalmist, mentioned his bones in the Bible when he was in trouble or pain. Once, when he was very sad, he wrote, "*Have mercy on me, Lord, for I am faint; heal me, Lord, for my bones are in agony*" (Psalm 6:2). In another Psalm, often attributed to David, the writer says, "*For my days vanish like smoke; my bones burn like glowing embers*" (Psalm 102:3).

At times, when David was deep in sin and was confessing those sins to God, he referred to his bones. Here are two examples. "*When I kept silent (before I confessed) my bones wasted away through my groanings all day long*" (Psalm 32:3 AMP). "*Because of your wrath there is no health in my body; there is no soundness in my bones because of my sin*" (Psalm 38:3).

These scriptures clearly show that David needed God's healing for his bones, healing that was physical, emotional, and spiritual. When he received restoration, he expressed his gratitude by saying, "*I shall be joyful in the Lord, I shall rejoice in His deliverance. All my bones shall say, 'Lord, who is like you?'*" (Psalm 35:9-10 ESV). Today, my goal is to make you think about how to have healthy bones, in a scriptural sense. David has already given us one way: we confess our sins and then let God forgive and cleanse us.

Here's another daily requirement for our bones.

> *"Trust in the Lord with all your heart and lean not on your own understanding; in all your ways submit to him and he will make your paths straight. Do not be wise in your own eyes; fear the Lord and shun evil. This will bring health to your body and nourishment to your bones."*
> —Proverbs 3:5-8

The Amplified Version says, "*It will be health to your nerves and sinews, and marrow and moisture to your bones.*" Now, that's a picture of healthy bones!

A third necessity for healthy bones is found in Proverbs 17:22. "*A cheerful heart is good medicine, but a crushed spirit dries up the bones.*" If we don't want dry bones, we need cheerful hearts. If we don't have these, we can turn to God's word to find out how to get them. *The Amplified Bible* translates the word blessed as "happy, fortunate, and enviable," and the Bible describes a person with a happy or cheerful heart as one who:

- relies on the Lord for help and is confident in him.
- lives by the godly wisdom found in God's word.
- is kind and merciful to the poor.
- reverently worships the Lord.

For healthy bones, we need cheerful hearts and minds. There are plenty of scriptures about our minds, but I'd like to recommend one for this week. Paul told us how to keep our minds in a cheerful or happy place when he wrote these words, "*Finally, brothers and sisters, whatever is true, whatever is noble, whatever is right, whatever is pure, whatever is lovely, whatever is admirable—if anything is excellent or praiseworthy—think about such things"* (Philippians 4:8). If we follow this advice from Paul, we will be well on our way to being cheerful.

We want to keep our bones healthy, and we don't want to be bone-heads. So let's get some back bone and bone up on God's word. Let's confess our sins and let God cleanse us. Let's trust God and keep our confidence in him alone. Let's seek a happy heart and a cheerful mind. We can do it! The Bible tells us so!

chapter twenty-nine

Heaven on Earth

Lots of things are described as "heavenly." Some years ago Chock full o'Nuts was advertised as the heavenly coffee. There's Angel Soft bathroom tissue, which I suppose means it's heavenly. There's even a candy called Heavenly Hash (although I happen to think all varieties of chocolate are pretty heavenly). Today I want you to tell you about Biblical truths regarding the heavens.

Genesis 1:1 teaches us the first truth. "*In the beginning God created the heavens and the earth.*" That's pretty clear. God made the heavens. Here's another fact about the heavens: they belong to God. "*The heavens are yours, O Lord, and yours also the earth; you founded the world and all that is in it*" (Psalm 89:11). So we have no doubt about the owner and founder of the universe.

The heavens tell the whole world about the glory of God.

> "*The heavens proclaim the glory of God. The skies display his craftsmanship. Day after day they continue to speak; night after night they make him known. They speak without a sound or word; their voice is never heard. Yet their message has gone throughout the earth, and their words to all the world.*"
>
> —Psalm 19:1-4 NLT

The heavens, according to the Bible, do not say, "Isn't nature wonderful?" They declare, "How glorious is our God!"

What God has created should lead us to believe in the creator. "For ever since the world was created, people have seen the earth and sky. Through everything God made, they can clearly see his invisible qualities—his eternal power and divine nature. So they have no excuse for not knowing God."

—Romans 1:20 NLT

That's pretty straightforward, isn't it? Paul writes like a Texan and tells it like it is!

Scripture verses about the heavens are wonderful. Whole books are written on the subject, but I'd like to focus on just three points.

1. *"For we know that when this earthly tent we live in is taken down (that is, when we die and leave this earthly body), we will have a house in heaven"* (2 Corinthians 5:1). Jesus said that he has prepared a place for us. Believe me – it isn't a little cabin tucked into a remote corner of eternity. Jesus said his father's house has many mansions, and that's where we will have our eternal home.

2. *"Who dares accuse us whom God has chosen for his own? No one— for God himself has given us right standing with himself. Who then will condemn us? No one—for Christ Jesus died for us and was raised to life for us, and he is sitting in the place of highest honor at God's right hand, pleading for us"* (Romans 8:33-34). We have someone in heaven pleading our case for us, interceding for us. That's so comforting. We know how weak and unclear our prayers can be, but we know that Jesus explains us to the Father and speaks on our behalf.

3. *"Store your treasures in heaven, where moths and rust cannot destroy, and thieves do not break in and steal"* (Matthew 6:20). Heaven is where we should heap up our treasures. I'm sure we all have different ideas of what those treasures are. I suggest that they include the first and best of everything we have: our time, our talents, and our money.

Sometimes we give God our leftovers, and that's not much of a treasure. Give little, get little. How much time do we give him? Five minutes before we go to sleep, we say a few words to our Lord... then, oops, we fall asleep. God didn't even get five minutes. We might give our greatest efforts and considerable talents to worldly projects and social activities, which often promote self instead of God. Then we give a little to him, but we expect a deep relationship with him in return. Sometimes we are stingy with our monetary gifts as well. But when we give much to the Lord, we are investing in eternity.

We take pride in our birthplace, in our home state, our home country; but Paul writes in Philippians that we are citizens of heaven. As citizens here, we need to have passports in order to go to faraway places. Do you have your passport ready for heaven? Your name may be on it, but remember that the identifying picture is one of Jesus. He is the only way to get there.

We have a heavenly father, a heavenly calling to believe in him, a heavenly home, and the assurance of being brought safely into his heavenly kingdom. Now that's what I call heavenly!

chapter thirty

Freebies

God's kingdom works exactly opposite to the world's system in many ways. In the world, we often get because we earn, receiving because we deserve. Much of the time we can even earn our own way.

That's not how God's kingdom works. His kingdom works on the gift system. I can hear your thoughts. They're the same as my husband Bert's, "There's no such thing as free. If you get it for free, somebody else paid for it." This is true, especially in the Christian world. Somebody else paid for all we get from God. Jesus did, with his death on the cross. He paid it all. "*The wages of sin is death, but the gift of God is eternal life through Jesus Christ our Lord*" (Romans 6:23).

Our loving, all knowing God knew we could never earn our own way into his kingdom with good works or by being completely good, so he set up the free gift way. It's just free. Salvation and a daily relationship with God is free for the taking. Why don't we all take the free gift? Many times it's because we don't want to give up control. We don't really know the God to whom we need to surrender. We're afraid he'll ask us to do things we don't want to do. What if he sends me off somewhere to be a missionary? What if he doesn't want me to have my home, my car, my money—my own way? "No thanks," we think. "I'll stay in control."

You think you're in control, right? Let me ask you a question, "How's that working for you?" In the first chapter of the Old Testament book of Haggai, the people were in control of their lives. They were building up their homes, earning a living, and concerning themselves with their own needs, their own wants, and their own problems. The trouble was that God had told them to rebuild his temple. Unfortunately, their minds were on the worldly system, not on the spiritual system. They were focused on themselves, not on God.

This is what God said to them,

"Give careful thought to your ways. You have planted much, but harvested little. You eat, but never have enough. You drink, but never have your fill. You put on clothes, but are not warm. You earn wages, only to put them in a purse with holes in it."

—Haggai 1:5-6

Then God told them to go into the hills, get timber and rebuild his house. It was time for a change in focus and priorities.

Folks, we need to be about the business of our Lord. Our first need is to build our spiritual lives with the free gifts God has given us, instead of yearning for more earnings and forgetting him.

Matthew 6:33 tells us to make God's kingdom, his ways and plans and his righteousness, our first concern. Then he will take care of our needs. Work for God's company, his kingdom. The wages are great, and the retirement plan is out of this world. After we have accepted his free gift of eternal life and acknowledged that we want his control over our lives, we must use what we've been given to do right, to be right.

Paul reminded Timothy not to neglect the spiritual gifts he had been given. This is important advice for all of us. Besides the free gift of salvation and new life in God's kingdom, we have been given many other gifts. The world may call them talents or natural abilities, but they're gifts from God. Once we begin to pay attention to God's ways, we realize that we've been given those gifts to bless others. We may think, "Hey! I'm out of work. I can't give," or "I'm old, I can't do that," or "I'm a busy person with no extra time. I've got nothing to contribute." Nothing? Think about it. We all have gifts.

- Are you a gifted listener? Then listen. So many people need someone to hear them.
- Are you a giver? Do it cheerfully.

- Are you a good host or hostess? Invite people into your home.
- Are you a cook? Take a meal to someone ill or in need.
- Are you blessed with time? Pray. Pray for your country, your family, yourself, your friends, or the people on the church's prayer list.

Listen for what God says to do. Write a letter, feed the homeless, care for a child. Who knows what door he will open? God meant it when he said, "*Give and you will receive. Your gift will return to you in full—pressed down, shaken together to make room for more, running over, and poured back into your lap*" (Luke 6:38 NLT).

Maybe you're thinking, "There are too many needs. I can't make a difference." Some of the nuns working with Mother Teresa were overwhelmed by the needs around them. When they came to her asking what they could give to the destitute and dying, she answered, "Give them a smile."

We all have to start somewhere. Share yourself, your faith, and your encouragement. We don't work on a payday system. We work on a gift system, because that's what God does. God's gifts to us, and our gifts to others, aren't earned. They're given out of love. That's the way God wants it.

chapter thirty-one

Faith Comes by Hearing

When things aren't going our way, when tragedy strikes and when times are tough, we may feel as if we're losing our faith in God. It's easy to think our faith is just slipping away. Maybe. But maybe we're just having a pity party. (I have those sometimes, don't you?) Often God will step in and remind us of what to do. It's as if he says, "Where is your faith?" That's when we need these verses: Proverbs 4:20-23 says,

"My son, pay attention to what I say; turn your ears to my words. Do not let them out of your sight; keep them within your heart; for they are life to those who find them and health to one's whole body. Above all else, guard your heart, for everything you do flows from it."

What comes out of our hearts? Jesus said, "*The mouth speaks what the heart is full of*" (Matthew 12:34). We find out what's in our hearts by listening to what they say, by noticing what we say. If our hearts are full of God's words, his truth, then that's what will come out of our mouths.

"*Faith comes from hearing, and hearing by the word of Christ*" (Romans 10:17 NASB). What does that mean? I've heard the Word for sixty years, so why does my faith wax and wane? Well, folks, there's hearing and there is really hearing.

As a teacher, I learned that the more ways I presented a concept or truth, the more likely it was that my students would grasp it. I tried to get my students to hear what I was teaching, but also to see it, speak it, and apply it. God is doing the same thing in these scriptures. Since faith comes by hearing and by the Word of God, we need God's Word through the ears and the eyes and the mind in order to get it into our hearts. We have to guard our hearts so the truth can't leak out, and falsehood can't get in. Then God's words can flow confidently out of our mouths.

What comes out of our mouths is really important. Jesus said we would be both justified and condemned by our words, so good words should come out of our mouths. There are no neutral words. Words are either positive or negative. I remember an old song by Johnny Mercer called "Ac-Cent-Tchu-Ate the Positive," and that's exactly what we need to do. We need to speak the good all of the time.

Maybe we should be like the young man who rode his bicycle across a university campus. A passerby saw the message on the front of the young man's tee shirt announcing his occupational goal. It read, "I am going to be a doctor." As the cyclist rode on, the passerby noticed a sign on the rear of the bicycle. It read, "I am going to be a Mercedes."[14] Seriously now, while those are positive words, the truth of God's Word is not about getting things or having a life of ease. We're going to have troubles, tragedies and heartaches. We live in a fallen world with human beings. What are we seeking? We're seeking a strong, confident and consistent faith—faith in Almighty God, faith that carries us through anything and everything.

Our confessions matter. What are our confessions? This is important. The Latin word for confession means, "to say the same as." Therefore, we should confess, or say the same thing as, what God says in his Word. (That same Word which we have heard and seen and put in our hearts.) We need to let our faith be activated by his words.

For example, if we're feeling afraid, we can turn to Psalm 56:11, "*In God I trust and am not afraid. What can man do to me?*" The Bible is full of verses we can rely on when we are afraid. It's always a good idea to read the scripture verses surrounding the one that holds the promise. Often it tells us there's something we need to do or to know in order to receive the promise. Reading out loud can increase our understanding and make the verse stick in our memory. As we see the words and hear the words, we let them into our hearts.

Faith comes by hearing. Now that's a great promise. If we don't have faith or we experience a time of doubting, we needn't worry. Faith comes. It comes by hearing, and hearing by the Word of God.

We hear the Word going into our ears, and keep it before our eyes as we read it. We get it into our hearts as we think and meditate on it. When it goes deep into our hearts, faith is produced.

So, one more time. How does faith come? By the Word of God.

chapter thirty-two

Kicked Forward

I once heard someone say he had so many problems that he wished Noah had built the *Titanic* instead of the Ark. That's a bit extreme. We all have bad days and troubles in our lives, but today I want us to think about the Apostle Paul and the problems he had during his life. And he had plenty! In 2 Corinthians 11:24-27, we find a list of some of the difficulties he experienced.

1. Given thirty-nine lashes five different times
2. Beaten with rods on three occasions
3. Stoned once
4. Shipwrecked three times
5. Adrift on the open sea for a whole night and a day
6. Exposed to danger from flooded rivers, robbers and those who hated him
7. Denied needed sleep
8. Plagued by hunger and thirst
9. Cold because he lacked proper clothing

From other references, we also know he was imprisoned and most likely had some sort of ongoing physical problem.

Pretty horrible, right? What was Paul's response to these troubles? Did he give up? Did he feel sorry for himself? Did he blame God? Did he feel that God had deserted him? No. Here are two of his responses. One is found in Philippians 4:13 (AMP),

"I have strength for all things in Christ who empowers me. (I am ready for anything and equal to anything through Him who infuses inner strength into me. I am self-sufficient in Christ's sufficiency)."

Another response is in Romans 8:37 (AMP). Paul says that amid all suffering and hardship, we are *"more than conquerors and gain a surpassing victory through Him Who loved us."*

If Paul had quit, if he had lost his faith in God's power because of his difficulties, we would be missing ten books of the New Testament. But Paul knew a secret about his strength. Paul had a "thorn in the flesh." No one knows for sure what it was. He begged God to take it away, but God's response was, *"My grace is all you need. My power works best in weakness."* Then Paul said,

"So now I am glad to boast about my weaknesses, so that the power of Christ may work through me. That's why I take pleasure in my weaknesses, and in the insults, hardships, persecutions, and troubles that I suffer for Christ. For when I am weak, then I am strong."
—2 Corinthians 12:9-10 NLT

Isn't that encouraging? We all know our weaknesses. We have clear views of our problems. Nevertheless, we must let ourselves be strong in the Lord. We can be. God never tells us to do something that he doesn't give us the power to do—if we choose to do it. Ephesians 6:10 from *The Amplified Bible* says, *"Be strong in the Lord (be empowered through your union with Him); draw your strength from Him (that strength which His boundless might provides)."*

Four of Paul's letters were written when Paul was a prisoner in Rome. Martin Luther translated the Bible while forced to hide in a German castle. John Bunyan wrote *Pilgrim's Progress* while in prison in Belford, England. Dietrich Bonhoeffer wrote monumental Christian literature from a concentration camp. What might God do with us, if we use our misfortunes to draw close to him?

Dr. E. Stanley Jones wrote this about the Apostle Paul: "If Satan was to buffet him, then Paul would determine the direction in which the blows would take him. Forward! Sometime ago, when I got into the back seat of a friend's car, the front seat passenger remarked, 'My seat needs to come forward a little, but it seems to be stuck. Kick it forward.' I obliged, and as I did I was reminded that this is precisely what life does to one who wants to be like Jesus. Life may kick him, but he determines the direction he goes after he is kicked: forward."[15]

I want to choose that direction, forward, don't you? Sometimes we do get stuck spiritually and need to be kicked forward like that car seat. People who have lived as long as I have know this is the truth. It's during the difficult times of life that we get kicked forward. Those are the times we draw closer to God.

When Paul wrote that he had the strength for all things through Christ, he was in prison. Still, he knew that God was using him and empowering him. Nothing can happen to us that won't "kick us forward," if we are determined to depend on and trust in our loving, heavenly Father. I can just see us as big ol' strong Christians, strong in the Lord, making the devil cringe when we say, "Go ahead! Make my day! Kick me forward!"

chapter thirty-three

A Level Praying Field

I love a good joke. The best are the ones that make me say "Oh yeah! I know how that feels," or "I never knew anyone else ever did that or felt that way." We humans are much more alike than we are different. For example, what do you think about while singing a hymn or praise song in church? Hopefully, you think about the Lord. But if, on occasion, your mind wanders, have you ever asked yourself any of these questions?

- What's for dinner?
- When does the football game start?
- Who's that singing off-key behind me?
- Why don't we ever sing my favorite song?
- Did I turn off the curling iron?
- Will there be doughnuts after the service today?

Admit it! Nearly all of us have had a few of those thoughts. I'd love to know some of your thoughts. I'll bet I've had some of those, too. One of my children, who shall remain nameless, said he (or she) wondered what it would be like if frogs jumped out of the baptismal bowl. I must admit I've never had that thought.

Even though we are a lot alike, we have our differences. To compensate, society often tries to create an even playing field. For example, remember the way kids choose up sides for a game? The best players get chosen first for each team, creating more even talent pools for each side. Everybody I know claims to have felt the pain of being the last one chosen. I certainly did.

We can also be tempted to think that the "Praying Field," or the spiritual playing field, is uneven—that we are not on the same level, so to speak, as others, or that we might get picked last by God. Not true! God has made the field level and all of us equal in his sight. Let's remind ourselves from his Word that we're all the same in his eyes. We are dealing with an equal opportunity God.

- *"For God so loved the world...that whoever believes..."* (John 3:16). We all receive his love. We are all "whoevers."
- *"But God demonstrates his own love for us in this: While we were still sinners, Christ died for us"* (Romans 5:8). When we come to him, when we accept his love, we all receive the same forgiveness and mercy.
- *"The Lord...is patient with you, not wanting anyone to perish, but everyone to come to repentance"* (2 Peter 3:9). Somehow we fall into two ways of thinking about God's ability and willingness to forgive us. We're either too good to truly need it, or so bad that it couldn't possibly work. Listen! Sin is sin, and we can't enter into heaven with a single bit of it. We all need forgiveness.

I love this story about "a little bit of sin." Two teenagers wanted to see the latest movie, one their father was quite sure was inappropriate.

"There's only a little bad language in it," they pleaded. "There's almost no violence, and, while they talk about sex, you never see any on screen." The father was adamant. The teens were upset. Eyes were rolling. Grumbles were rumbling. But this was a very creative dad who loved his children and wanted to make a point. He headed to the kitchen to bake a batch of brownies. The house was filled with the tantalizing aroma of the coming chocolate treat. The teens soon made their way to the kitchen, begging for brownies.

"Help yourself!" the father said, "But before you dig in, you should know that I added just a little bit of dog poop to the recipe. There's not much. You won't be able to see it. I'm pretty sure you won't even taste it. It probably won't hurt you a bit. So go ahead. Have all you'd like."[16]

They got the point. That's the way sin is in our lives. It doesn't matter how much or how little, it's still there.

First John 1:10 says, *"If we claim we have not sinned, we make him (God) out to be a liar and his word is not in us."* Fine! But how about those of us who have really messed up? Some of us have had this thought, "I've done so much wrong, really evil stuff. I know I'm beyond redemption, beyond forgiveness." Not true! Those who are forgiven for much love him all the more. None of us are beyond his forgiveness.

We are on a level field. God offers all of us the same love and the same forgiveness. God equally desires each of us to be his own. He searches for us and joyfully receives us. We are like the lost coin in the parable that Jesus told. Let me recount it for you.

> *"Suppose a woman has ten silver coins and loses one. Doesn't she light a lamp, sweep the house, and carefully search until she finds it? And when she finds it, she calls her friends and neighbors together and says, 'Rejoice with me; I have found my lost coin.' In the same way, I tell you, there is rejoicing in the presence of the angels of God over one sinner who repents."*
>
> —Luke 15:8-10

The lost coin in this scripture was a silver drachma. It was probably only the size of a dime, but its value was about a day's wages. It was worth the search. And we are worth the search. If we're feeling lost, either eternally or temporarily, we can be sure that God desires to find us and to help us find him.

We have a level praying field: same love, same forgiveness, same Father who desires to find us every day. Next time you see a dime, let it remind you to cry out, "Here I am, Lord. You've found me."

chapter thirty-four

Marvelous Mercy

I grew up in the foothills of the mountains of Western North Carolina, where we had some special ways of talking. Where I'm from you could say anything bad or critical about anybody as long as you said, "Bless their hearts" first. It sounded something like this.

- "Bless his heart, he never did have the brains God gave a grasshopper."
- "Did you see that outfit Edna Mae wore to church last Sunday? Bless her heart, you know she must be color blind."
- The worst thing you could say was, "Bless his heart, you know he's a Yankee."

That sort of talk truly spoils God's idea of blessing someone, doesn't it? The other word we used in the same critical way was the word "mercy." We completely ruined the Biblical concept of mercy whenever we wanted to gossip this way:

- "Lord have mercy, she looks like a hussy. You'd think she'd have better sense than to wear her clothes so tight."
- "Lord have mercy, was that Deacon Jones coming out of that liquor store?"

Sometimes we shortened "Lord have mercy" to "it's a mercy" or "for mercy's sake," or, if we had a lot to say and were in a hurry, just plain "mercy."

- "It's a mercy he hasn't had a wreck, the way that boy drives."
- "For mercy's sake, you know they don't have the money for that new car. They're going into debt again."
- "Mercy, don't tell me they're starting another building fund at our church. What do they do with all that money? It's always money, money, money."

But here's the truth. No matter how we misused the words, we are blessed and God's mercy is a really good thing. In fact, it's not just good, it's marvelous.

I heard a story about a Sunday school teacher who was encouraging her class of young adults to become fully surrendered to God. Suddenly, one of the students raised her hand and complained, "But if I do surrender everything to God, I'll be at his mercy!" Exactly. I want to assure you that "at his mercy" is right where we want to be.

Mercy can mean compassionate treatment of an enemy or prisoner. God gives us compassion when we put ourselves under his power. Mercy can also be defined as kindness beyond what is expected or fair. God provides that as well. Because Christ has paid the penalty for our sins, God gives us mercy instead of justice. Merciful people are inclined to forgive. That describes God, too. It's a good thing, because we all need his forgiveness.

How do we know God is merciful? In Exodus, when Moses was on Mt. Sinai to receive the Ten Commandments, God appeared and described himself as, "*The God of compassion and mercy...slow to anger and filled with unfailing love and faithfulness*" (Exodus 34:6 NLT). God called himself merciful.

Mercy was a favorite topic of David's. In the King James Version of Psalms we read:

- "*Have mercy on me, and hear my prayer*" (Psalm 4:1).
- "*I have trusted in thy mercy*" (Psalm 13:5).
- "*Goodness and mercy shall follow me all the days of my life*" (Psalm 23:6).
- "*I will be glad and rejoice in thy mercy*" (Psalm 31:7).
- "*Great is thy mercy toward me*" (Psalm 86:13).

- *"The Lord is good; his mercy is everlasting"* (Psalm 100:5).

David certainly knew God was merciful, that he needed God's mercy, and that he could ask for it and receive it. So can we, not because of any goodness in us, but because mercy is one aspect of God's character. His very nature is to be merciful. Remember, he declared it of himself.

You've heard the expression, "Throw yourself on the mercy of the court." People who do that know they're guilty. They know they're not asking for what they deserve or for justice. We do that with God. We throw ourselves at his feet in his court, at his throne. This is what Hebrews 4:16 says, *"Let us then approach God's throne with confidence, so that we may receive mercy and find grace to help us in our time of need."*

We receive mercy, and so we must give it. Jesus said, *"Be merciful, just as your Father is merciful"* (Luke 6:36). Marvelous mercy! Let's accept God's mercy. God is kind and loving. He knows all things and is all-powerful. Yes, we want to be at his mercy. It's a wonderful place to be.

chapter thirty-five

September 11, 2002

It's such a privilege to meet together today, to commemorate those who died in the terrorist attacks last year, and to honor those who have shown such courage and sacrifice in the wake of the tragedy.

While watching television this week, I saw part of a program about NORAD. That stands for the North American Aerospace Defense Command. This program, set in place many years ago, is designed to detect and intercept any air invasion coming in from outside our nation—missiles, planes, etc. The narrator of the show pointed out that on September 11, 2001, the system was working perfectly, but it was of no help to our nation. Our country had expected an attack from without, but this one was from within. Of course, attacks from within are more insidious, more frightening, and much more difficult to detect and defend against.

Since 9/11, we have seen the implementation of various kinds of security systems for our protection: airport security, immigration checks, Social Security number checks and more demand for photo ID's, to name a few. But I'd like to tell you about another kind of system. As people who belong to God, we can be a real asset to our country's security against terrorism.

1 Timothy 2:1-2 says, *"I urge, then, first of all, that petitions, prayers, intercession and thanksgiving be made for all people—for kings and all those in authority, that we may live peaceful and quiet lives in all godliness and holiness."* We can contribute to our country's security by following Timothy's urging, by praying for our leaders. That's our first defense against whatever would destroy our freedom to live in peace and godliness.

Jesus said in John 8:12, "*I am the light of the world.*" He is the light our country needs for guidance. When we sing "God Bless America," we evoke God's blessings on our country and ask to be guided by him, for he is the light from above. But in Matthew 5:14, 16, Jesus said, "*You are the light of the world...Let your light shine before others, that they may see your good deeds and glorify your Father in heaven.*"

I suggest that the second way in which we can help keep our country secure is to live out that verse. *The Amplified Bible* version of Matthew 5:16 tells us how to shine ..."*with moral excellence and praiseworthy, noble, good deeds,*" not for our own glory, but for the glory of God. Our world needs "the light from above," and we, as God's people, are to reflect that light. The world is looking for the light through good, noble, love-filled deeds.

Tonight I hope you will take time to remember all who died in the attacks and to honor the courage and sacrifice that has been shown by so many. Then, pray for the world, our country, and for all in authority. Ask God for a country of peace and godliness. Offer praise that Jesus is our light. And let's determine in our hearts, with God's help, to be lights to our family, our neighbors, our country, and our world by doing good deeds in Jesus' name.

chapter thirty-six

Magnification

A popular piece of advice is floating around the internet. You'll find it in posts about having a good attitude. It hails back to the early 1900's, though. "Keep your eye on the doughnut, and not on the hole." In other words, where is our focus? What we focus on is what gets magnified in our lives.

What occupies our time, our thoughts and our emotions? Do we focus on the people who have hurt us, offended us or "done us wrong"? Are we looking back on the unpleasant things that have happened to us? What should we do? Well, we can either get down in the dumps and stay there, blaming the world for all our misfortunes, or we can get out of bed every day and move forward as far as our feet will take us.

Jesus said, "*No one who puts his hand to the plow and looks back is fit for service in the kingdom of God*" (Luke 9:62). If a person who is plowing a field keeps looking back instead of looking ahead, he will surely plow some crooked rows. If we've accepted Christ as our Savior, but are forever looking backwards into the past, we're plowing some crooked rows too. Perhaps we haven't lost our faith, but we have lost our focus. Our eyes are on the hole instead of the doughnut.

When we focus on our pasts, our trials, our troubles, and our pain, we often make them bigger and more important than they really are. We magnify them. How can we stop doing that mess and get past the habit of exaggerating our troubles? (Yes, I know our troubles are real, but they don't need to define us.) Here's how we can change. We are to focus on Christ and his Word. I don't say that glibly. It isn't easily done, because we have two real enemies who don't want us to do it—the flesh and the devil. Both of those will fight us every step of the way. But that battle has already been won for us through the sacrifice made by Christ on the cross.

To focus means to set our eyes on one specific thing in order to make that image clear. Focusing requires that we concentrate our thoughts and efforts. This is the complete opposite of trying to multi-task or of trying to juggle many thoughts on a subject. When we focus on God and his Word, we are seeking a clear, distinct and sharply defined picture of what God has done for us. We want—we need—to physically, emotionally and spiritually magnify all of the great things God has provided for us. For starters:

He loves us.
He died that we might live.
He has taken our sin and given us his righteousness.

At one time in his life, David was a fugitive from his own country. King Saul was trying to kill him, so he went to the court of a Gentile king for refuge. However, that king suspected him of being an enemy. In order to save his own life, David feigned madness. He even scratched at the door and slobbered in his beard. How humiliating! What was David's reactions to his really terrible situation? Here's what he wrote at the time: Psalm 34:1-3 (AMP). The questions in parentheses are mine.

- "*I will bless the Lord* (When?) *at all times;*
- *His praise will* (How often?) *continually be* (Where?) *in my mouth.*
- *My life makes its boast* (In whom?) *in the Lord;*
- *Let the humble and the afflicted* (Do what?) *hear and be glad. Oh magnify the Lord with me and let us exalt His name together.*"

How do we magnify the Lord? A big part of doing that is thanking him for all things in every circumstance. In fact, we need to make a determined effort to be grateful during hard times. I can tell you that God has used hardship and pain to produce good in our lives. My personal testimony is that many times I didn't see the good until the hardship was over. But, when I do see his hand at work in my life in the midst of pain, the situation ends more quickly and is easier to bear. Slowly, we learn not to focus on the "hole," but to trust Romans 8:28, which tells us God is working things out for good.

We can't let our thanksgiving be based on our feelings (which can change more quickly than the weather) or on our circumstances (which are never dependable). Once we learn to focus on God, there's always a reason to give thanks. We can begin to look away from the things that bother us or bring us pain and turn instead to eternal things, the truths that will matter forever. That's when we are better prepared to receive God's blessings.

So, where should we focus? What shall we magnify? Let me leave you with this verse.

"Let all who seek You rejoice and be glad in you; And let those who love Your salvation say continually, 'Let God be magnified,'" (Psalm 70:4 NASB).

chapter thirty-seven

The Barnabas Bunch

D o you remember the nursery rhyme about Humpty Dumpty? Sometimes, I too feel the need to be "put back together again." We don't really need all the king's horses and all the king's men. What can often help restore our wholeness, though, is a hearty dose of sincere encouragement.

Acts 4:36-37 tells of a man named Joseph who sold a field and brought the money to the apostles. He encouraged the early church so much that they nicknamed him Barnabas, which means Son of Encouragement. Barnabas lived up to his name. When Paul came to Jerusalem, many of the apostles were afraid he was a fake and didn't want to meet with him. (Remember, he had been hauling Christians off to prison pretty recently.) Barnabas, however, encouraged them to accept Paul, explaining the change God had made in Paul's life.

When a report came that the people of Antioch had begun to believe in Jesus, Barnabas was sent to them. The Bible says he encouraged the believers to stay true to their faith and to the Lord. Then he encouraged Paul to come to Antioch to teach. In Antioch believers in Jesus were called Christians for the first time. Barnabas was indeed a great encourager. We can be too. I'd like to invite you to join my new club. It's called The Barnabas Bunch. Here are the by-laws for our organization.

1. We promise not to give prideful encouragement by building ourselves up or by saying, "If you'd do what I did ..." If we find that we're proud, we will zip our lips. Sometimes we know, or think we know, exactly what someone should do.

We may be very tempted to share our considerable knowledge with a superior attitude. But 1 Corinthians 8:1 says, *"Knowledge puffs up while love builds up."* (So no puffin' allowed.)

2. We promise not to be insincere. We will not build up and tear down at the same time, sort of like the old southern cliché of saying something rotten but ending the sentence with "bless her heart." (For example, her gravy has more lumps in it than an old mattress, bless her heart.) We will concentrate on words that really do build others up.

3. We promise to consider these questions before giving encouragement: Will it help develop faith and hope? Does it promote peace? Is it spoken in love? Will it bless the person receiving it? Will it build the person up without tearing anyone else down?

Paul describes the perfect attitude of an encourager in Romans 15. He wanted to resolve a disagreement among the believers about a regulation that was causing a rift in the fellowship. He instructed them to stop passing judgment on each other, to stop doing anything that caused distress to a fellow believer. He told them to focus on pleasing God, living in peace, and encouraging one another. He described how we are to encourage each other this way.

"We who are strong ought to bear with the failings of the weak and not to please ourselves. Each of us should please our neighbors for their good, to build them up" (Romans 15:1-2).

Here's how that works. Each of us has different strengths and weaknesses. You can bear with my doubts and fears and weaknesses and use the strengths you have in those areas to encourage me. In turn, I use my strengths where you may be weak to build you up. We do this, not to please ourselves, but to show our love for each other. And it's God who gives us the ability to be encouragers, even as he encourages us.

"For everything that was written in the past was written to teach us, so that through the endurance taught in the Scriptures and the encouragement they provide we might have hope. May the God who gives

endurance and encouragement give you the same attitude of mind toward each other that Christ Jesus had, so that with one mind and one voice you may glorify the God and Father of our Lord Jesus Christ. Accept one another, then, just as Christ accepted you, in order to bring praise to God."

—Romans 15:4-7

If you agree to the three by-laws listed, then welcome to the Barnabas Bunch. Here's the club motto. (I hope you'll memorize it and say it often.)

"Therefore, encourage one another and build each other up" (1 Thessalonians 5:11).

Activate your new membership by encouraging someone today. You'll find you are encouraged yourself as you help someone else. May God make each of us sensitive to the needs of others and use us to express his love.

chapter thirty-eight

Mounds of Treasure

I have a son-in-law who is Greek. His mom, Helen, was a great cook, and made wonderful cookies with names that I can't pronounce. Once, when Helen was making cookies with our granddaughter, they got to the part of the process where the hot buttery treats needed to be coated with powdered sugar. But Helen had specific instructions for Elizabeth. She explained, "You don't need just a sprinkling of the white stuff on these. You have to put on *mounds* of sugar." The finished product was supposed to be heaped up with powdered sugar, ready to delight those eager to eat them.

The Bible talks about mounding or heaping up—not powdered sugar, of course, but other things that are much more important.

> *"Do not gather and heap up and store up for yourselves treasures on earth, where moth and rust and worm consume and destroy, and where thieves break through and steal. But gather and heap up and store for yourselves treasures in heaven, where neither moth nor rust nor worm consume and destroy, and where thieves do not break through and steal. For where your treasure is, there will your heart be also."*
> —Matthew 6:19-21 AMP

Most of us spend a lot of effort and time trying to store treasure, as in money, on earth. One of my very wise sons-in-law says that, with regard to the human condition and earthly treasure, "More is never enough." So, I want to change our focus today from earthly treasure to heavenly treasure. I don't believe that what we think of as treasure is what God considers treasure. What are some of the heavenly treasures God wants us to mound up in heaven?

"My child, listen to what I say and treasure my commands. Tune your ears to wisdom, and concentrate on understanding. Cry out for insight, and ask for understanding. Search for them as you would for silver; seek them like hidden treasures."

—Proverbs 2:1-4 NLT

'Sounds to me as if the Word of God says to seek wisdom and understanding as diligently as we do financial security. Where can we find that wisdom?

"In him (Christ) lie hidden all the treasures of wisdom and knowledge" (Colossians 2:3 NLT). God couldn't make our way more clear, could he? We must get better and better acquainted with Jesus and his teachings. In him we will find wisdom and knowledge.

"In the house of the uncompromisingly righteous is great, priceless treasure" (Proverbs 15:6 AMP). Our righteousness is only through Christ. None of us are in right standing with God except through Jesus, but we must do what is right and not compromise with the world or with Satan's agendas. We are responsible for standing firm in Christ. Every time we choose to do what is good and right instead of what is evil or wrong, we heap up treasures in heaven.

Isaiah 33:6 (AMP) reminds us that, *"the reverent fear and worship of the Lord is our treasure and His."* That's a wonderful verse. As we stand in awe of God and worship him, we are enriched and so is he. Imagine that! Sometimes we ask, "What can I do for God?" Often we're only thinking in terms of good works, but this verse suggests that we do for him by worshiping him. So this begs the question, have we got a mound of worship stored up in heaven?

Finally, our treasure in heaven, begun on earth and continuing for all eternity, is our salvation through Jesus Christ. You're going to love this passage from the New Living Translation:

"All praise to God, the Father of our Lord Jesus Christ. It is by his great mercy that we have been born again, because God raised Jesus Christ from the dead. Now we live with great expectation, and we have a priceless inheritance—an inheritance that is kept in heaven for you, pure and undefiled, beyond the reach of change and decay. And through your faith, God is protecting you by his power until you receive this salvation, which is ready to be revealed on the last day for all to see. So, be truly glad! There is wonderful joy ahead, even though you must endure many trials for a little while."

—1 Peter 1:3-6 NLT

- Our salvation is a treasure in heaven.
- Being Christians is not for wimps.
- Heaping up in heaven requires firm faith and works.

When you see a mound—an ant mound, a Mounds candy bar, or a cookie covered in mounds of sugar, think about the mounds in heaven that you are heaping up, mounds of:

- wisdom
- understanding
- uncompromising righteousness
- faith tested by sacrifice and suffering
- glory
- honor
- praise
- and eternal life

All these are stored in heaven for us by the mercy and grace of God. What a treasure—a treasure far more important than any we may acquire on earth!

chapter thirty-nine

Coloring Book Prayers

There was a cartoon in the newspaper recently of a family praying the Lord's Prayer together. When they said, "Give us this day our daily bread," the little girl in the family added, "with the crust cut off, please."

It occurred to me that I often pray like that little girl. I seem to be trying to dictate to God what I think he should do for me and for those for whom I pray. I draw him a picture of what I want and then ask him to sort of color in the lines according to his will. (After all, I really can't boss God around, can I?) But maybe I should suggest what colors I want him to use. Sometimes I even want to add numbers, prioritize things a bit, so that God will know where to start and how to proceed. I call this a "coloring book prayer."

Coloring book prayers are not a new problem. There's a parable in the Bible that Jesus told in Luke 18:10-14.

> *"Two men went to the Temple to pray. One was a Pharisee (a religious leader of the Jews and a strict follower of the law), and the other was a despised tax collector. The proud Pharisee stood by himself and prayed this prayer, 'I thank you God that I am not a sinner like everyone else. For I don't cheat, I don't sin, and I don't commit adultery. I'm certainly not like that tax collector! I fast twice a week, and I give you a tenth of my income.'*
>
> *But the tax collector stood at a distance and dared not even lift his eyes to heaven as he prayed. Instead, he beat his chest in sorrow, saying, 'O God, be merciful to me, for I am a sinner.' I tell you, this sinner,*

not the Pharisee, returned home justified before God. For those who exalt themselves will be humbled, and those who humble themselves will be exalted."

I've been like that Pharisee. I've heard myself pray, "Why this, Lord? I've worked in the church. I read my Bible. I've not done bad things. I, I, I!" Verse nine of that chapter, right before the parable, states that Jesus was talking to people who trusted in themselves, only in themselves. I bet they drew God lots of prayer pictures, trying to convince him that not only did they know what they needed and when, but also that they deserved it.

Paul wrote that he and his traveling companions had been through all kinds of trouble in Asia. *"We were crushed and overwhelmed beyond our ability to endure, and we thought we would never live through it. In fact, we expected to die.* (Ever felt that way?) *But as a result, we stopped relying on ourselves and learned to rely only on God, who raises the dead"* (2 Corinthians 1:8-9). It seems to me that the focus of our prayer life needs to be taken off what we feel (and what we think and what we want) and placed on God and who he is, so that we can trust him.

You know these "I'll draw you a picture, God. Please color it as I desire," prayers are not pleasing to God's ears. We're treating him as our servant, as a Fairy God Father, to fulfill our wishes, like a celestial vending machine. That is so upside down. We are his people. We are his servants.

So, how do we change? We are told to ask, seek and knock. We're instructed to make our request known to him. The answer, then, is to focus more on God and who he is by remembering to whom we are praying. He is:

- The Creator of the World
- King of the Universe
- The All-powerful God
- The All-knowing Lord
- The All-faithful Father
- The God who made the mountains, and who can move them if necessary

- The God who has been faithful to us and wants to use us in his kingdom
- The one who wants the best for us
- The God who loves us

We won't spend so much time drawing our pictures for God to color, or dwelling on how and when he should answer our prayers, if we remember what God said in Isaiah 55:8-9, "*My thoughts are nothing like your thoughts…And my ways are far beyond anything you could imagine. For just as the heavens are higher than the earth, so my ways are higher than your ways and my thoughts higher than your thoughts.*"

We can take great comfort in those words if we decide to trust God more than we trust ourselves or anyone else. Let's do it. Let's take that leap of faith. That leap is really just a whole bunch of baby steps of faith, taken day after day.

If I could, I would reach out from these pages just now and give you a box of crayons to remind you that God has all the colors that ever existed. He created them all. He is a much better artist than we are. We don't need to tell him how to draw or how to color. We can make our requests known to him and then trust him for the best answers, for the most beautiful picture, and for our best life.

chapter forty

Always

In a marriage seminar, I learned to avoid using the words never and always when arguing with my husband Bert. The teacher gave these "he said/she said" examples:

- She says, "You **never** listen."
- He says, "You **never** stop talking."
- She says, "You **always** leave your underwear on the floor."
- He says, "You **always** burn the toast."

A fellow teacher of mine called those glittering generalities, and I agree that we shouldn't use them. The Bible, though, has some very good advice for us, using the word always.

First, let's consider Luke 18:1 from *The Amplified Bible. "Jesus told them a parable that they ought always to pray and not turn coward (faint, lose heart, or give up)."* There's our first always verse for today. In a recent email, I was encouraged to PUSH, which stands for "Pray Until Something Happens." Always pray. We may think, "I've prayed. Nothing happened. Maybe I'm not praying the right way." But God says, "Don't faint. Don't stop." Keep believing that God will do what he knows is best for us. When fiery darts of doubt attack our prayer life, we can hold up that shield of faith that says, "Your will be done," without fear, because we know God loves us.

The prayer life of Jesus is our perfect example. He prayed all the time. He acknowledged God the Father in everything he did. He prayed alone, but he also prayed with and for others. And (great news!) he prayed for us. In John 17:20, we find Jesus praying for those who followed him on earth, saying "*My prayer is not for them alone. I pray also for those who will believe in me through their message.*" Jesus is praying for us. What better encouragement can we have to always pray?

Another always is found in Philippians 4:4. "*Rejoice in the Lord always. I'll say it again; Rejoice.*" *The Amplified Bible* adds, "*Delight, gladden yourself in Him.*" Most of us look to someone other than ourselves to make us glad. How can we gladden ourselves? Think about the word rejoice. "Re" means to go back, return to a previous state, again, anew or over again. When we don't feel like rejoicing, or when we think we have nothing to be happy about, we need to recycle our joy in Christ by remembering what he has done for us. For starters:

- He died for our sins.
- Because of him we have eternal life.
- He has promised to be with us, to help us, to deliver us from trouble.

The Bible is full of great promises. Find one. Be glad about it. We can get our joy back. We can Re-Joy. Let's start by thanking him for everything. If we recall our blessings, joy will return. Rejoice always.

Finally, in 1 Thessalonians 5:15, we find, "*Make sure that nobody pays back wrong for wrong, but always strive to do what is good for each other and for everyone else.*" Paying back evil for evil involves many things. Someone hits us, we hit back. 'Doesn't help. In sports, it's usually the guy who hits back that gets the penalty. The refs almost never see the first blow. Not hitting back isn't enough, though. If we don't hit back, we may still be full of resentment, waiting to retaliate, holding a deep, ugly grudge. That's no way to live. We keep thinking we're right and they're wrong. What they did just burns us up. Yes, it does burn *us*, but that hatred (of course, we never call it that) or resentment doesn't burn *them* at all.

Holding a grudge, trying to get even with someone who has wronged us, is like the farmer who wanted to torture the chicken hawk who had been killing his chickens. He caught the hawk and tied a stick of lighted dynamite to it. He let it go, ready to delight in its demise. The hawk flew into the farmer's barn. You can imagine the end of the story. The resulting fire burned down the whole barn and killed the rest of his chickens. We must abandon resentment and grudges, and do some serious forgiving. Jesus tells us to forgive as we have been forgiven. For me, that's a lot of forgiving. Instead of evil for evil, we are always to do good to fellow believers and to everyone else.

We can give money, time, talents, emotional support, or physical support. We can give smiles, kind words, encouraging words, praise, and hope. We can tell our story of what God has done for us. Are you shy and unsure of what to say? I understand. Many years ago, I took a course called Evangelism Explosion. I was so intimidated by the concept that when we would make house calls to witness to people, I prayed that no one would be at home. Be not dismayed, we shy folks can still be evangelists. I Peter 2:1 reminds us to live in such a way that unbelievers simply see our good works and then, because of them, glorify God. Actions can speak louder than words.

Maybe you're sitting there thinking, "Sounds good, Beth, but I really don't believe I have the power, time or talents to do good deeds—at least not many of them. That just can't be my way of life." Well, Ephesians 2:10 says otherwise. *"We are God's handiwork, created in Christ Jesus to do good works, which God prepared in advance for us to do."* We are **created** to do good works. They are in us, and we are able to do them. Therefore we are without excuse if we don't do the good works we can do.

How often we hear ourselves say, "There's nothing I can do." Or "I just don't know what to do." The Bible tells us what to do. Always pray, always rejoice, and always do good.

Hold Fast

When I taught high school, a quick and easy way to decorate my classroom was with clever, catchy posters. I remember one depicting a cute but terrified kitten, clinging to a small tree branch by his two front paws. His hind legs were dangling in the air. The caption read, "Hang in there!"

We've probably all said those words to someone and assumed them to be encouraging in a vague sort of way. My husband, Bert, got an email just this week from an old high school friend who closed his note with, "You folks hang in there and enjoy." That was kind of nice. He meant, "Don't give up. Keep on keeping on." But have we ever stopped to think about what we really should be hanging on to?

The Bible says, "Hang in there." Well, actually, it says, "Hold fast." Better still, it tell us exactly what to hold fast to. If that poster's kitten lets go of the branch, he's in big trouble. We can stay out of trouble (or get out of trouble we're already in) by clinging to—holding fast to—the right things.

"*Test everything that is said. Hold on to what is good*" (1 Thessalonians 5:21 NLT).

Nearly every day, we're bombarded with bad news, strange opinions and stories of sinful behavior. God's word says, "hold fast"—look at, consider, and believe what you know is good. Look for the good and cling to it. How do we do that? 1 Thessalonians 5:22 is the perfect place to start, "*Reject every kind of evil.*" We don't have to allow ourselves to be sucked in by lying, lust, greed, gossip—any kind of evil. If we do, then we aren't holding fast to what is good.

The Message is a contemporary paraphrasing of the Bible. Here's how it presents Philippians 4:8. *"Summing it all up, friends, I'd say you'll do best by filling your minds with and meditating on things true, noble, reputable, authentic, compelling, gracious -- the best, not the worst; the beautiful, not the ugly; things to praise, not things to curse."* The best, the beautiful, and the praiseworthy things: if our minds are filled with these, we are holding fast to what is good.

Then 1 Timothy 1:19 (NLT) says, *"Cling to your faith in Christ, and keep your conscience clear. For some people have deliberately violated their consciences; as a result, their faith has been shipwrecked."* We know when we're deliberately violating our consciences, don't we? We choose to think and do wrong things. Like what?

- We view or listen to what we called "dirty stuff" when I was a kid. (Now I guess the dirty has progressed to filthy or obscene.)
- We choose to be cruel, to say a hurtful thing rather than an encouraging one.
- We hold on to an offense, rather than forgiving.
- We neglect our relationship with God. Prayer and Bible reading lose out to TV, exercise, house cleaning, web surfing, the latest novel, or an extra hour of sleep.

When we violate our consciences, we damage our faith. I saw a cartoon in the newspaper recently. It showed a young girl explaining to her brother, "Conscience is a little voice inside your head, but sometimes it just whispers." We must listen carefully to hear that little voice, because the world is so loud. Our conscience is like a compass. The Word of God is our life's map. So, if we're feeling lost, we need to look at our compasses and consult our maps.

In 2 Timothy 1:13-14 (AMP), Paul writes, *"Hold fast and follow the pattern of wholesome and sound teaching which you have heard from me, in the faith and love which are in Christ Jesus. Guard and keep the precious and excellently adapted [Truth] which has been entrusted [to you], by the [help of the] Holy Spirit Who makes His home in us."* Carefully guarding and holding fast to our faith and doing what is loving sure takes some hard work and action on our part. We can't just sit back and let Satan and the world roll over us. Faith must have an impact on our behavior.

Finally, look at Hebrews 10:23-24 from the New Living Translation. *"Let us hold tightly without wavering to the hope we affirm, for God can be trusted to keep his promise."* The Bible is full of wonderful promises. Find some that apply to your life and to your needs. Read them in context, pray them, and then hold fast to them, because God is faithful and can be trusted.

We may be tempted to say, "Well, I don't see anything happening." Hold fast! Let's not dwell on – or rehearse in our minds, emotions, and spirits – what isn't happening yet. Let's rehearse, repeat, lean on, and hold fast to the certainty that God is faithful. Even when we do that, we'll have times of doubt. But don't worry: God understands. We can feel free to say to our loving, powerful, and wise Savior, "Help us, Father, to hold fast. By your Holy Spirit in us, help us not to doubt. We do believe. Help us to overcome our unbelief."

So, whenever we hear the words, "Hang in there," we can be reminded to hold fast. Hold fast to what? Hold fast to what is good, to faith, to a clear conscience, to wholesome and sound teaching, to our confession in Christ Jesus, and to our hope in him and in his faithfulness.

Don't let go!

chapter forty-two

Juicy Fruit

L et me begin today with something funny. A kid sees a farmer coming down the road.

Kid: Hey! Whatcha got in the wagon?
Farmer: I've got me a load of manure.
Kid: Whatcha gonna do with that manure?
Farmer: Well, I'm gonna spread it on my strawberries.
Kid: Wow! You ought to come to my house. We put whipped cream on ours.[17]

I love fruit (especially with whipped cream). But don't you just hate to bite into a beautiful red strawberry and find it's all mushy inside, or peel a banana only to discover that it's mostly bruises? Have you ever thumped about a dozen watermelons and still wound up with a tasteless one? We know how fruits are supposed to taste, and can be disappointed when they miss the mark.

Knowing when a watermelon is juicy and sweet just by looking at it is impossible, but God says we can know what people are like by looking at their fruit. And he expects to get fruit from us. Here's a Bible verse that's almost a little scary.

"Early in the morning, as Jesus was on his way back to the city, he was hungry. Seeing a fig tree by the road, he went up to it but found nothing

on it except leaves. Then he said to it, 'May you never bear fruit again!'
Immediately the tree withered."

—Matthew 21:18-19

What if Jesus comes looking for our fruit? How many times do people come to us hungry for love, patience, goodness, kindness, encouragement, or any other kind of help, and we give them a leafy show—platitudes, a quick fix idea, or any other response with no real substance. Religious bumper stickers and cross necklaces aren't the way to show ourselves as Christians. We need to be ready with real fruit from the Holy Spirit himself. Galatians 5:22-23 gives us a list of those fruits: love, joy, peace, patience, kindness, goodness, faithfulness, gentleness, and self-control.

Is it really possible for us to show that kind of fruit? Yes! If we belong to God, we can bear fruit for him. Jesus said we do that by staying connected with him, focused on him, and submitted to him. He used a parable about gardening to explain, saying,

"I am the true vine, and my Father is the gardener. He cuts off every branch in me that bears no fruit, while every branch that does bear fruit he prunes, so that it will be even more fruitful... No branch can bear fruit by itself; it must remain in the vine. Neither can you bear fruit unless you remain in me"

—John 15:1-5

Later in the same chapter, Jesus says that his true followers produce plenty of fruit, thereby bringing glory to God.

All this truth is wonderful, but how do we apply it to our lives in a practical way? I know that the fruit of the Holy Spirit is produced by the Spirit, but it doesn't just pop out of us unless we take some action. So, let's explore possible actions in relation to each of the fruits of the Spirit listed earlier.

1. How can we exhibit love today? 1 John 3:18 says, *"Dear children, let us not love with words or speech but with actions and in truth."* For example, don't say, "Honey, I can sure tell you're

127

tired. I love you for cleaning the house today," as you plop down on the couch to read or watch T.V. Instead, take out the garbage, do the supper dishes, give the kid his bath, and clean up the bathroom when you're finished. Love is something we do.

2. How can we show joy despite our circumstances? Do something to make someone else happy. Stay focused on the good things in life. You're overcome with worry? Go play catch with your son, bake cookies with your daughter, or get everybody involved in a game of Monopoly.

3. Can we be at peace? Many times we're not able to let the Holy Spirit produce peace in our lives because we need to forgive someone or apologize to someone. Do it! Take action, especially if you think the person you're angry with doesn't deserve it.

4. Can we be patient and even tempered? Think of some of the traffic situations you face. Let the Holy Spirit work. Don't grumble and fume about the guy who keeps changing lanes or the old lady who drives under the speed limit. The best way to remember to be patient is to remember that we're not perfect either.

5. Can we offer kindness? Are we easy to get along with? We'll be more kind if we remember that, "there but for the grace of God, go I." Why not allow the frazzled mother of the crying baby in the supermarket to go ahead of you in the line?

6. Can we demonstrate goodness? Only God is perfectly good, and we need to trust his goodness in order to do good things for others. Be good by listening to someone, praying for them, or even giving small gifts when possible. Remember, little things mean a lot.

7. Can we demonstrate faithfulness? Being faithful means never giving up and keeping our word and our promises. It means committing ourselves to God and his plans and then hanging on forever. It requires us to quit being wishy-washy in our

walk with God by believing only when it's convenient or studying and praying only when our schedule permits.

8. Can we demonstrate gentleness and humility? These are the opposite of pride and of the attitude that our way is the only right way. We can take action in this area by realizing we're as human as the other guy. Why not give others credit, affirmation, and compliments for a change? God hates pride, but loves a humble spirit.

9. Can we demonstrate self-control? We do this by consistently making right choices. Many times, maybe most of the time, we know what we should do. Now we need to let the Holy Spirit drive us to do it. The more we get to know God and his love, the more we'll want to make the right choices.

Can we demonstrate the fruit of the Spirit? The Bible says we can, because the Holy Spirit lives in us. We can be those vines that abide in Christ Jesus, vines filled with sweet fruit, ripe and ready for use in God's kingdom.

chapter forty-three

Punching Holes in the Darkness

Some time ago I read about an incident in the boyhood of the author, Robert Louis Stevenson. Put to bed quite early one evening, he passed the time looking out the window, watching the lamplighter as he lit the gas street lamps. Robert's mother came into his room and asked him what he was doing. He replied, "I'm watching the man punch holes in the darkness."

Truly, the greatest hole ever punched in the darkness of our world, in all of history, was the birth of Jesus Christ. He is even called the Light of the world. And he loves us! Isn't it pleasant to just sit and bask in that light, in that wonderful truth? Ah, but we can't get too comfortable. Just sitting is not God's plan for those of us who have accepted him as Savior and Lord. Take a look at Matthew 5:14-16 from *The Amplified Bible.*

> *"You are the light of the world. A city set on a hill cannot be hidden. Nor do men light a lamp and put it under a peck measure, but on a lampstand, and it gives light to all in the house. Let your light so shine before men that they may see your moral excellence and your praiseworthy, noble, and good deeds; and recognize and honor and praise and glorify your Father who is in heaven."*

If we are to be lights, let's think of ourselves as such. What can we do to punch holes in the darkness? We should start in our own homes. This may sound strange, but a great deal of light would come upon our families if we would just stop, look, and listen to them. We try to work on the computer, talk on the phone, and answer our child's or mate's question all at the same time. We women are masters of multitasking, yet how many times have we said, "Please, look at me when I'm talking to you." We need to look at our loved ones and let them see that they're important to us, more important than a computer, telephone, super bowl game, or a clean house, more important than things. In my case, I need to remember that they're more important than a black velvet skirt. I'll tell you a story.

Many years ago, when my granddaughter Elizabeth was six years old, we were all in church together. It was Christmas time and I had a new black velvet skirt. Elizabeth tiptoed up to where I was sitting and asked to sit on my lap. Without even explaining that I didn't want to mess up my wonderful, new, precious black velvet skirt, I said, "No." Well, the Holy Spirit used the hurt look on that child's face to convict me forever of the truth: "People are more important than things." I pray she doesn't remember the incident, and that I'll never forget it. The lesson bears repeating. People are more important than things.

People need our lights, they need for us to punch holes in our dark world. We have endless opportunities to do that.

- Give a frazzled clerk a smile, a compliment, a peppermint—especially if she makes a mistake or is oh, so slow.
- Let someone go in front of you in line. I guarantee you God will give that bit of time back to you later.
- Bake or buy a gift for someone who would never expect it.
- Take children to a nursing home or a retirement home. The residents love to see children. Let the children sing for them.
- Write a special note thanking a missionary for punching holes in the darkness where you cannot go.
- Hug a whole bunch of people. You never know who needs a hug.
- You've got more ideas of how to shine. Just remember that *things* do not see Jesus. *People* see Jesus.

Sometimes, we begin to feel "punched out." We may be thinking, "I'd like to do these things, but I'm not shining very brightly right now.

I'm tired and busy, and I've got problems of my own. I have my own darkness to deal with." Where do we go for oil for our lamps? We get to go to the source of all light, a Light that no darkness can ever extinguish.

- *"In him was life, and that life was the light of all mankind. The light shines in the darkness, and the darkness has not overcome it"* (John 1:4-5).
- *"The Lord will be your everlasting light"* (Isaiah 60:19).
- *"For with you is the fountain of life; in your light we see light"* (Psalm 36:9).
- *"Your word is a lamp for my feet, a light on my path"* (Psalm 119:105).

God punches holes in our own darkness so that we can share his love with others. He's the light of the world, and has asked us to punch holes in the darkness for him.

chapter forty-four

Refreshment

I love York Peppermint Patties. I remember a campaign of TV commercials that all started with the words, "When I bite into a York Peppermint Pattie, I feel…" What followed was a series of the most refreshing scenarios one could imagine. I want you to be refreshed today, not with candy, but with the Word of God.

Refreshment can be equated with relief (as from heat or thirst), renewed strength (as from food and drink and rest) or replenishment (of whatever we are lacking). You and I could use all those facets of refreshment in our lives, especially spiritually. Let's take them one at a time.

Relief. This is covered in a spiritual way in Acts 3:19 (AMP). "*So repent (change your mind and purpose); turn around and return [to God], that your sins may be erased (blotted out, wiped clean), that times of refreshing (of recovering from the effects of heat, of reviving with fresh air) may come from the presence of the Lord.*"

Renewed strength. Here's what Jesus said, "*Let anyone who is thirsty come to me and drink*" (John 7:37). Unless we drink from the Water of Life, Jesus, we will thirst forever, never refreshed. Jesus also called himself the Bread of Life. Jesus is our bread, and Jesus is the Word (according to John 1:1). Often refreshment and help come to us from his Word precisely when we need it.

Once I was very nervous about flying to Europe. Yes, I prayed about it, but I was really scared. Here's what I found in the Bible that freed me from that fear. "*If I rise on the wings of the dawn, if I settle on the far side of the sea, even there your hand will guide me, your right hand will hold me fast*" (Psalm 139:10). Those were the words I needed, right when I needed them. God helped me with his Word. I was refreshed! And he'll do the same for you.

Replenishment. Sometimes we just need a new supply of strength or wisdom or any number of things. Philippians 4:19 (ESV) promises that, *"God will supply every need of yours according to his riches in glory in Christ Jesus."*

Think about new supplies for strength and power. Take a look at Isaiah 40:31 from *The Amplified Bible.* This verse tells us how to receive the supplies we need. *"But those who wait for the Lord [who expect, look for, and hope in Him] shall change and renew their strength and power; they shall lift their wings and mount up [close to God] as eagles [mount up to the sun]; they shall run and not be weary, they shall walk and not faint or become tired."* Replenishment comes to those who expect, look for, hope in, and draw close to God.

Refreshment can also be related to revival of our memory or a renewed mind. The Bible tells us very clearly how to have a renewed mind and what a new mind brings into our lives. Paul wrote,

> *"And so, dear brothers and sisters, I plead with you to give your bodies to God because of all he has done for you. Let them be a living and holy sacrifice—the kind he will find acceptable. This is truly the way to worship him. Don't copy the behavior and customs of this world, but let God transform you into a new person by changing the way you think. Then you will learn to know God's will for you, which is good and pleasing and perfect."*
> —Romans 12:1-2 NLT

Note, please, that our part is to submit to God. His part is to change the way we think, to renew our minds. He even sent us his Holy Spirit about whom Jesus said in John 14:26, *"But the Advocate, the Holy Spirit, whom the Father will send in my name, will teach you all things and will remind you of everything I have said to you."* God has fully provided for a revived memory.

Spiritually, we can be fully refreshed in every way by our Lord God. So next time you bite into a mint, have a drink of water, eat some food, get some rest, have a need met, or remember a blessing, think about God. Praise him for your refreshment. Anytime we need to be refreshed, let's go to God, to his Word, and to prayer. We'll come away washed clean, watered, fed, rested, supplied, and clear-headed.

chapter forty-five

All Grown Up

We often ask our children, maybe just to make conversation, "What do you want to be when you grow up?" What if God asked us, "What do you want to be now that you are grown up? I don't mean your occupation, what you do. I mean what you are all the time."

With a sincere heart, but perhaps a bit piously, we might answer, "Oh, God, I want to be a person filled with love, joy, peace, patience, kindness, goodness, faithfulness, gentleness, and self-control."

"Why that sounds just like what I created you to be," God might answer. "I even had Paul write these characteristics down for you in Galatians 5:22. These are the fruit of my Spirit. Have you made any plans for becoming the person you described?"

"Well, God, I do try. I work really, really hard at it. I do as many good things as I can, and I make every possible attempt not to do bad things."

Suppose God asked, "How's that working for you?"

For many of us, our answer might be, "Honestly, it isn't working."

"Well, child," God has already said through the Bible, "let me tell you some good news. Apart from me you can do nothing. With me all things are possible. If you want this good fruit, you must be planted in the right place."

In light of that conversation, let's examine where our roots are planted. These verses are taken from *The Amplified Bible*. Look at Colossians 2:6, "*As you have therefore received Christ…*"

What does that mean, to receive Christ? John 1:12 (AMP) explains it very well. "*But to as many as did receive and welcome Him, He gave the authority (power, privilege, right) to become the children of God, that is, to those who believe in (adhere to, trust in, and rely on) His name."* That's what receiving Christ means, to believe he is the Son of God and to have faith in him.

Okay, back to Colossians 2:6-7. Verse six tells us what to do. *"As you have therefore received Christ, [even] Jesus the Lord, [so] walk (regulate your lives and conduct yourselves) in union with and conformity to Him."* Verse seven tells us how to do it, tells us how we can conduct our lives in accordance with God's will. Here's how. *"Have the roots [of your being] firmly and deeply planted [in Him, fixed and founded in Him], being continually built up in Him, becoming increasingly more confirmed and established in the faith, just as you were taught, and abounding and overflowing in it with thanksgiving."*

Where do our roots need to be planted? In Christ. That's the only place where we will grow, the only source of that good fruit we want.

The first fruit of the Holy Spirit in Galatians 6:22 is love. Maybe all the other fruits are contingent on that one growing in us first. From my concordance, I found 186 references to love in the Bible, 117 of them in the New Testament.

These verses say, among other things:

- God so loved the world.
- Love your enemies.
- Love your neighbor as yourself.
- Abide in God's love.
- God is love.
- Nothing can separate us from the love of God.
- People will know we are God's disciples if we love each other.

Romans 5:8 tells us that, *"God shows and clearly proves his love for us by the fact that while we were still sinners, Christ died for us."* That's quite different from what we often think. We reason, "If I can just clean myself up, stop sinning, do things right, then God will love me." Wrong! He loved us first!

1 John 4:19 adds that, *"We love because he first loved us."* Doesn't that show us that we can trust his love? We didn't earn it, so we can't lose it.

We didn't earn it, so we can't take credit for it. We can't produce love. Christ produces it in us, when we are rooted in him.

I'll close with part of the prayer Paul wrote in Ephesians 3:16-19 (NLT),

> *"I pray that from his glorious, unlimited resources he will empower you with inner strength through his Spirit. Then Christ will make his home in your hearts as you trust in him. Your roots will grow down into God's love and keep you strong. And may you have the power to understand, as all God's people should, how wide, how long, how high, and how deep his love is. May you experience the love of Christ, though it is too great to understand fully. Then you will be made complete with all the fullness of life and power that comes from God."*

May Christ make his home in our hearts! Only then will the fruit of the Spirit be produced in our lives so that we can be what we want to be, now that we're all grown up... deeply rooted in Christ and in his love.

chapter forty-six

Deep Roots

This is what you might call an interactive lesson, so if you're game, stop reading and go grab a sheet of paper and a pen or pencil (or, if you want to be really creative, a couple of crayons.) Today, I want to talk about roots again. Go ahead and draw the trunk of a tree. Okay, done? No more drawing for now.

In Isaiah 37:31, God said of his people, *"Once more a remnant of the kingdom of Judah will take root below and bear fruit above."* They were to take root downward first, and then bear fruit above. Isn't that just common sense? I think God wanted to remind us that we need roots before we get fruit, that lots of activity takes place where it can't be seen. Any gardener will tell you that roots do plenty of growing underground, often before you and I see anything going on above the dirt.

We identify what people are by their fruit. Matthew 7:16-17 says,

"By their fruit you will recognize them. Do people pick grapes from thornbushes, or figs from thistles? Likewise, every good tree bears good fruit, but a bad tree bears bad fruit. A good tree cannot bear bad fruit, and a bad tree cannot bear good fruit."

We know we want good fruit, but how do we get it? No roots, no fruits. Imagine ourselves as trees that need good roots. Jesus said, "I am the vine; you are the branches. *If you remain in me and I in you, you will bear much fruit; apart from me you can do nothing"* (John 15:5). To bear fruit, we must be connected to the vine, Jesus. He is our own taproot, the main root out of which our support roots spread. Go ahead and draw a long root straight down from your trunk. Label it Jesus.

What are some of those roots that spread out because of Jesus? We looked at this verse last week. *"So then, just as you received Christ Jesus as Lord, continue to live your lives in him, rooted and built up in him, strengthened in the faith as you were taught, and overflowing with thankfulness"* (Colossians 2:6-7). Out of our taproot, Christ, we see faith and thankfulness, more strong roots to hold us firmly and to keep us grounded. Draw those two roots out from the taproot. Label then faith and thankfulness.

"Withstand him (the devil); be firm in faith [against his onset—rooted, established, strong, immovable, and determined], knowing that the same (identical) sufferings are appointed to your brotherhood (the whole body of Christians) throughout the world" (1 Peter 5:9 AMP). Through our faith in Christ we are rooted deeply enough and strongly enough, and we are determined enough, to resist the devil and to endure hardships. Draw out of the root of faith two more roots. Label them resistance to evil and endurance of hardships.

Christ said, *"Produce fruit in keeping with repentance"* (Matthew 3:8). Part of our root system must include a root that turns from sin and asks for forgiveness. God promises that when we ask, he'll forgive. And just as we are forgiven, we are to forgive. Now, that we've covered roots of repentance and forgiveness (both received and given) it's time for more artwork. Out of the root of thankfulness, draw two more roots, and label them repentance and forgiveness.

I love Psalm 1:2-3, *"but whose delight is in the law of the Lord, and who meditates on his law day and night. That person is like a tree planted by streams of water,* (Some versions say "firmly planted," meaning it has deep roots.) *which yields its fruit in season and whose leaf does not wither—whatever they do prospers."* If we want those promises of fruit, unwithered leaves, and prosperous maturity, we must first, as part of being connected with the tap root of Christ, delight in the Lord and meditate on his word. Draw two more roots out of the taproot. Label them "delight in Christ" and "meditation on God's Word."

Connected to the vine, our root system includes faith, thanksgiving, resistance to evil, endurance through hardship, commitment to meditation on God's Word, delight in the Lord, repentance, forgiveness received, and forgiveness given. Imagine all those things rising up in us.

- How? Through the Holy Spirit, who is God in us.
- Through what power? Love.
- Where did everything begin? With God's love. "For God so loved…"

I counted 117 verses on love in the New Testament, but I want to close with the same passage as last week, Ephesians 3:16-19, this time from the New International Version. It's a great passage for us to pray for ourselves. *"I pray that out of his glorious riches he may strengthen you with power through his Spirit in your inner being, so that Christ may dwell in your hearts through faith. And I pray that you, being rooted and established in love, may have power, together with all the Lord's holy people, to grasp how wide and long and high and deep is the love of Christ, and to know this love that surpasses knowledge—that you may be filled to the measure of all the fullness of God."* We are rooted in the soil of God's love, with Jesus as our taproot and the indwelling power of the Holy Spirit strengthening and maturing us.

Oh, that we might be good, deeply rooted, stately, upright, useful, stable, durable, incorruptible trees, trees that bear much fruit for God's kingdom and for his glory.

chapter forty-seven

Rope of Hope

I've seen a bumper sticker that says, "When you come to the end of your rope, tie a knot and hang on." 'Not a very pretty picture—swinging in the air, hanging onto the end of a rope. So, here's a better idea. When you come to the end of your rope, let go and grab on to God's rope of hope. I want to tell you about one of the times (and there have been many more) when God provided me hope. Maybe some of you are in need of hope today.

Years ago, our youngest daughter gave birth to her first child, a nine pound, one ounce boy. It was a long labor with no pain-killers. Mother and father were doing fine, but Baby Jake had a problem. He was whisked away to the neo-natal intensive care unit before Becky and Michael even got to hold him or get a good look at him. He was put on oxygen, an IV for antibiotics, and four monitors of various types. All this was scary for young parents and for old grandparents.

What do we always say in difficult times? "I hope everything will be okay." But we're human. We have fears, dread, discouragement and negative thoughts that come from time to time. But, as God's children, we also have a strong rope of hope, a lifeline that can pull us out of those kinds of emotions and thoughts. I suggest that the rope of hope is made up of five strong strands woven together. We can hold on to every one of them.

First, our hope is in God. *"But now, Lord, what do I look for? My hope is in you"* (Psalm 39:7). God is always on our side and is ready to help in times of trouble.

Secondly, our hope is made strong by the Word of God. His Word has the power to squelch those negative, fearful, and discouraging words that we hear from the world, or from our own doubting, or from Satan. *"Everything that was written in the past was written to teach us, so that through endurance taught in the Scriptures and the encouragement they provide we might have hope"* (Romans 15:4). We need to read those scriptures that will help us stay in hope, verses like these:

> *"Wait and hope for and expect the Lord; be brave and of good courage, and let your heart be stout and enduring."*
> —Psalm 27:14 AMP

> *"Behold the Lord's eye is upon those who fear Him (who revere and worship Him with awe), and wait for Him and hope in His mercy and loving- kindness."*
> —Psalm 33:18 AMP

A third strand in the rope of hope is prayer. We must pray and get others who love God to pray also. My daughter, Brenda, suggested that, in our baby's situation, we should pray the prayer of relinquishment taught by Catherine Marshall. A powerful prayer, it goes something like this:

> *"Dear heavenly Father, how I want to trust you, even when I don't feel the truth of what you've said in your Word! You've promised that you're always with me, that you love me, and that you know what's best for me. So now, regardless of any feelings or emotions stirring around inside me, I choose to give this whole situation to you. I trust you. I accept your will in this matter, whatever the outcome may be, because you are all-knowing and all-powerful. Hold me to this decision, Lord, even when my emotions say otherwise. Thank you, Lord. I praise you for all that you are and all that you do. Amen."*[18]

God. His word. Prayer. The fourth strand in the source of hope is friends and family who love God. My best friend, my husband Bert, said, "Remember the goodness of God. Think of all the things he has brought us through in our 46 years together." Yes, think and talk about his goodness. A friend from Bible study helped me so much by suggesting that we pray John 9:3 for Baby Jake, that *"this happened so that the works of God might be displayed in him."* God can use hard times in our lives to display His works.

Our son Brad reminded me that God is sovereign, the supreme authority over everything. Yes! We serve a God who doesn't bring fear or evil, but one to whom we can joyfully submit, because his supreme authority is manifested by his extravagant love.

The final source of hope I want to mention is the ministering of the Holy Spirit in our lives. God, the Holy Spirit, is our Helper, our Comforter and our Counselor. As I prayed for Jake, the Holy Spirit reminded me of a story found in Numbers, Chapter 13. Moses sent twelve spies into Canaan, the land God had promised to the Israelites. These men were to report on the land and determine whether or not the Israelites could conquer the people living there. Ten spies said it couldn't be done. The cities were too well-fortified, the men were like giants. But two, Joshua and Caleb, believing God's promise, gave a good report. They said they knew they could take the land because God would be with them. The good report! God the Holy Spirit used that account to remind me to believe every good report about our baby's progress and to refuse those doubts and fears that would storm into my head from Satan and the world (and the internet).

Everything outside of God seems to want us to be filled with fear. Even the weather station has programs about *The Most Terrifying Storms of the Century*. No! Don't go near fear. Believe the good reports. It's a battle, but we can do it. Fight off the "What if?" and the "I'll never." Refuse the fears that try to take over our thoughts. Instead, take only the good report of what God says about you and about what he will do for you. Wait with joyful expectancy. That's what hope is. Wait in hope.

Ecclesiastes 4:12 says *"A cord of three strands is not quickly broken."* We have a five-strand rope of hope. We have God, his Word, prayer, Christian friends and family, and the working of the Holy Spirit in our lives. That hope can keep us strong and steady. If we get discouraged this week, let's talk to ourselves and say with confidence Proverbs 23:18 "*There is surely a future hope for you, and your hope will not be cut off.*"

By the way, to God be the glory, Jake is now a happy healthy teenager. Hope on!

chapter forty-eight

You Reap What You Sow

D o you know the word *comeuppance*? The dictionary says it means "deserved punishment." Where I grew up in the foothills of Western North Carolina, it was a word used to mean "He's reaping what he sowed."

- If a man suffered a heart attack, you might hear someone say, "Well, what do you expect? All he ever did was work and worry. You reap what you sow."
- If a family had a problem with a child, the neighbors would whisper, "Well, you know, they never did discipline that boy. He was wild from the beginning. They sure sowed that seed."
- If someone had financial problems, the local response would be something like this, "I'm not a bit surprised. He made his money by overcharging everybody when he owned that furniture store over on Main Street. And, Lordy me, he'd repossess at the first hint of a late payment. He's just reaping what he sowed."

I'm a bit embarrassed to say that we enjoyed making such comments as these, especially if those getting their comeuppance were better off or higher up the social scale than we were. Sadly, I grew up looking only at the negative side of the Biblical truth, "*A man reaps what he sows*" (Galatians 6:7). The truth is, there's a wonderfully positive side to that spiritual law.

Here's what Galatians 6:7-10 says in *The New Living Translation*.

"Don't be misled—you cannot mock the justice of God. You will always harvest what you plant. Those who live only to satisfy their own sinful nature will harvest decay and death from that sinful nature. But those who live to please the Spirit will harvest everlasting life from the Spirit. So let's not get tired of doing what is good. At just the right time we will reap a harvest of blessing if we don't give up. Therefore, whenever we have the opportunity, we should do good to everyone—especially to those in the family of faith."

How do we reap the good harvest of blessings? We plant good seeds—not once or twice, but at every opportunity. What are those seeds? Doing what is good to and for others. We don't have time to cover all the good seeds that produce great harvests for us, so let's focus on the most important crop. It's the one listed as the first fruit of the Spirit, and it's the seed of the greatest commandment, love.

We know that love is something we do, so we start by doing loving things for others. Putting aside ourselves and what we want or need, we help with the dishes. We play with the kids. We baby-sit for another couple. We listen to someone else's problems (especially when ours are worse than theirs.) We drive a sick friend to the doctor. You get the picture. You know how to love. I know the truth of what I'm about to tell you. Been there, done that. I probably own the tee shirt.

If we've been "doing love" for a long time and don't see any signs of harvest, something's wrong. We need to examine our hearts for a real crop killer before we move on. That crop killer is usually unforgiveness. Someone, somewhere, sometime has hurt us—done us wrong. It could be just a small offense that we've nurtured until it's grown into something huge, or it could be something big, something horrible that's been done to us. There's only one answer for either situation. We must forgive.

Now, before you tune me out, consider this. To forgive someone doesn't mean that we approve of their actions, nor are we excusing what was done. We're not saying, "Oh, that's okay. Just forget it." We're simply making a choice to forgive the person and leave him in God's hands. Forgiveness is a choice, not a feeling. This is very serious business and vital to our relationship with God.

In Matthew 6:14-15, Jesus said, "*For if you forgive other people when they sin against you, your heavenly Father will also forgive you. But if you do not forgive others their sins, your Father will not forgive your sins.*" The longer we harbor unforgiveness, the deeper the root gets, and the more it affects our attitudes and our relationships. Let's examine our hearts for any unconfessed unforgiveness. Then, finally once and for all, confess it and give the person or situation over to God.

Remember, God is faithful to forgive us of the sin we confess and to cleanse us of it. Don't let the devil or your mind tell you, "You didn't really forgive. You don't feel any different."

Just say, "Oh yes I did! My feelings are up to God. I choose to forgive." Then we can do loving deeds, plant seeds of love, and reap a harvest.

- We can sow peace. We don't have to be right all of the time. We don't need to argue about everything.
- We can sow encouragement. We can look for the good in people and tell them about it. When our children do ten things right and one thing wrong, what do we talk about? (Yes, the one wrong thing, you and me both.) But maybe now we can focus on the right things that they do.
- We can sow patience. No, "they" do not need to do "it" right this minute.
- We can sow gentleness. The seeds of a soft answer, a tender word, a pat on the back, or a hug can help overcome an angry situation. Our world needs a bumper crop of this.

You can think of all kinds of good seed to sow. Before a farmer plants his seeds, he looks over his fields and decides what he needs—oats for his animals, wheat for bread, corn and beans for canning. Then he plants what he needs to reap. It's the same in the spiritual world. We plant into the kingdom what we need to harvest in our own lives.

Many years ago, I attended a women's Bible study that centered on improving marriages. (Deep inside, I felt that my husband Bert should be attending. Certainly, he needed it more than I.) I call the main points of the three-session seminar the "Triple A" system. We were to concentrate on adapting to, admiring, and appreciating our husbands. "Well, phooey," I thought, "now I know Bert should be doing it. He always gets his way. I'm the one who needs to be admired and appreciated." But I did the "Triple A" system. I planted those three seeds. And guess what! After nearly sixty years of marriage, Bert does the "Triple A" system better than I do. I may have sown the seeds, but, oh, what a healthy harvest God has produced for me!

Sometimes we may wonder if we are capable of planting good seeds. The Bible says we can.

"Grace abounds to us so that we can abound in good works."
—2 Corinthians 9:8

"For we are God's handiwork, created in Christ Jesus to do good works, which God prepared in advance for us to do."
—Ephesians 2:10

What we do might seem as small as little seeds, but our acts of love can produce a joyful harvest. What we sow, we shall reap.

chapter forty-nine

American Idols

Think back to your Play-Doh days for a moment. Today I want each of us to figure out whether we are molding, or being molded. (And I'm not talking about that stuff that grows in our shower stalls.)

God commanded us to put him first in our lives when he said, in the Ten Commandments, "*Have no other gods before or besides me. You shall not make yourselves an idol in the form of anything in heaven above or on the earth or in the waters below*" (Exodus 20:3-4). Are we shaping or molding any idols in our lives?

If you came to my house, you wouldn't see any carvings of stars or moons or animals or sea creatures on altars, ready to be worshipped. But I'm not entirely sure that I don't have some idols in my life that need to come down. A Bible teacher once told me that an idol is anything that's more important to me than God.

In our hearts, at the deepest place of our spirits, we would probably say, "There's nothing more important than God." But, in our day-to-day walk, do we live that truth? Are we molding any idols? When someone or something is loved and important to us, there's an old expression that says we put that person or thing on a pedestal. We need to look into our hearts and minds to see what we're "putting on pedestals." Those could be our idols.

In chapter 6, verse 24, of Matthew, Jesus reminded his followers that we can't serve two masters. We can serve God or we can serve mammon (which means riches, money, and possessions.)

Jesus also reminded us, in that same chapter, to stop worrying so much about our lives that we ignore God. Even what we eat, drink, or wear can become idols. If those things are more important to us than God, they are on our pedestals. We need those things, and God knows it. We don't have to worry about them. In Matthew 6:33 (AMP) Jesus assures us this way: "*Seek (aim at and strive after) first of all His kingdom and His righteousness (His way of doing and being right) and all these things will be given you besides.*"

There's a verse in the book of Jonah that continually pricks at my heart. It's in chapter 2, verse 8. It's part of Jonah's prayer from the belly of the fish. As he prays, he comes to this revelation and conclusion, "*Those who cling to worthless idols forfeit the grace that could be theirs.*" I wonder how much grace and loving kindness and blessing God would pour out on us if we would give up our idols and make him first in our lives, having no other gods before or besides him.

If we stop molding false gods, then God can mold us. Isaiah 64:8 gives us this prayer, "*Yet you, Lord, are our Father. We are the clay, you are the potter; we are all the work of your hand.*" Even though God's process of shaping us into what he wants us to be is painful at times, it's a good thing. Jeremiah 29:11 assures us that we're not haphazardly shaped or carelessly designed. God, the artist who molds us, has a perfect plan. He says so in this verse. "*'For I know the plans I have for you,' Declares the Lord, 'plans to prosper you and not to harm you, plans to give you hope and a* future.'"

God continually molds us so that his perfect plan, his will, can be fulfilled. Some of us take more work than others. Maybe we resist his shaping. Hard clay has to be kneaded—pushed and pressed to soften it and make it useable, pliable. This can be an uncomfortable process. The more quickly we recognize the potter's authority and his loving hand, the sooner he can mold us into what we are designed to be. This takes time. Fortunately, God doesn't give up on us. He is "*compassionate and gracious, slow to anger, abounding in love*" (Psalm 103:8).

We can love a lot of people. We can enjoy many things. But no person and no thing can become our God! You've heard of "cow tipping." We have some "pedestal tipping" to do. The question is, "What's on those pedestals?" What's keeping us from letting God be God, giving him the rightful place in our hearts? Let's let him mold us and make us into his people, people who can work in his kingdom.

"*Little children, keep yourselves from false gods—from anything and everything that would occupy the place in your heart due to God, from any sort of substitute for Him that would take first place in your life*" (1 John 5:21 AMP). How about it? Are we molding idols or letting God mold us? Frankly, I've got lots of gods to pull off their pedestals. Do you? I think we'd better get busy.

chapter fifty

The Rock

Long, long ago an old Indian chief was about to die, so he called for Geronimo and Falling Rocks, the two bravest warriors in his tribe. The chief instructed each to go out and seek buffalo skins. Several months later, Geronimo returned with 200 pelts, but, sadly, Falling Rocks was never seen again. The tribe never forgot him. Even today, as you drive throughout the West, you will see signs that say, "Watch out for Falling Rocks."[19]

If you like the comics, I bet you can tell me what Charlie Brown always gets in his trick or treat bag on Halloween. Yes, a rock, and then he says in his famously deadpan voice, "I got a rock."

I like funny stories. I also like rocks. I have one from an ancient fort in Honduras, and one from a glacier I walked on in Alaska. I picked one up in Greece at the site of the first Olympic Games, but happened to see a sign that removal of any rock or plant was prohibited. I put it back. My husband Bert is happy that I like rocks. They sure make for cheap souvenirs. Some women buy jewelry. I pick up rocks. Yes, I've reminded Bert that diamonds are rocks, but he didn't offer any for my collection.

Psalmists called the Lord God a rock many times.

- *"The Lord is my Rock, my fortress and my deliverer. My God is my rock, in whom I take refuge"* (Psalm 18:2).
- *"Turn your ear to me, come quickly to my rescue; be my rock of refuge, a strong fortress to save me"* (Psalm 31:2-3).

- *"My flesh and my heart may fail, but God is the Rock and firm strength of my heart and He is my Portion forever"* (Psalm 73:26 AMP).

When life is hard, when we are feeling low, depressed, confused, frustrated, or in pain, doesn't it seem as if we're walking through mud, slipping and sliding and trudging along? We begin to feel around for some firm footing, thinking:

- Maybe a good self-help book would offer a standing place.
- Maybe psychoanalysis.
- Maybe the counsel of a friend or two.

If that doesn't help, we try to hide the fact that we aren't standing very well. We hide behind drugs, alcohol, food, excessive spending, anger—lots of camouflage to hide the fact that our steps are shaky and our paths not firm. But here's the real answer to our dilemma.

"I waited patiently for the Lord; he turned to me and heard my cry. He lifted me out of the slimy pit, out of the mud and mire; he set my feet on a rock and gave me a firm place to stand" (Psalm 40:1-2). We need a firm foundation. We need the Rock. In Psalm 61:2, David cries out to God, pleading, *"Lead me to the Rock that is higher than I."* Good news! There is One who knows more about everything than we do. He can put us on the right, high, firm path. He'll do that because he loves us. We need the Everlasting Rock. No other foundation will do. When things all around us are crumbling, God is firm. 2 Timothy 2:19 (AMP) promises that, *"The firm foundation of God stands, sure and unshaken."*

My dad was a humorous, kind, and hardworking man. I loved him, and was blessed to know that he loved me. We were churchgoers, but Daddy often fell asleep during the sermon. In the superior attitude of my teen years, I wondered if he was really saved. Daddy always said, "People shouldn't talk about politics or religion. It always causes an argument. Just talk about fishing or pretty girls." So we didn't talk about church. Then one day I learned that Daddy's favorite hymn was

"The Solid Rock." From then on, I always knew where and how Daddy stood on faith.

My hope is built on nothing less
Than Jesus' blood and righteousness.
I dare not trust the sweetest frame
But wholly lean on Jesus' name.
CHORUS
When darkness veils his lovely face'
I rest on his unchanging grace.
In every high and stormy gale,
My anchor holds within the veil.
CHORUS:
On Christ the solid rock I stand.
All other ground is sinking sand.
All other ground is sinking sand.[20]

I hope you'll pick up a rock today and carry it in your pocket or purse, or maybe put it where you pray, or where you'll see it often. Let your little rock remind you of *the* Rock, the One upon whom we can stand firm. Christ is still the Rock and wants to be, as David declared him to be, our Savior, our Refuge, our Fortress, our Sanctuary, our Redeemer, our Deliverer, our Firm Strength, and the Cornerstone of our lives.

All other ground is sinking sand.

chapter fifty-one

Candy Canes

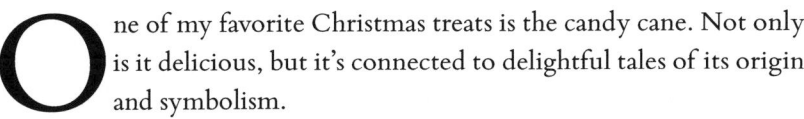

One of my favorite Christmas treats is the candy cane. Not only is it delicious, but it's connected to delightful tales of its origin and symbolism.

- One story says that in 1670 a choirmaster at the cathedral in Cologne, Germany, handed out sticks of sugar to his young singers to keep them quiet during the long Living Nativity Ceremony, bending them into shepherd's crooks in honor of the occasion.
- Another says that in 1847 a German-Swedish immigrant in Wooster, Ohio, decorated a small spruce tree with paper ornaments and white candy sticks.
- We do know that, around 1920, Bob McCormack began making candy canes as Christmas gifts for his friends and family, twisting and bending each piece by hand. The story goes that in the 1950's, a relative of Bob's invented a machine that automated the candy cane's production and made Bob's Candies, Inc. one of the world's largest producers of that Christmas treat.

I thought it would also be interesting to look at some of the Christian symbolism of the candy cane. Perhaps these will turn candy cane eating into a whole new experience.

The candy is indeed shaped like a shepherd's crook. Jesus said, "*I am the good shepherd; I know my sheep and my sheep know me—just as the Father knows me and I know the Father—and I lay down my life for the sheep*" (John 10:14-15). The Lord is our shepherd, and we are his sheep. What joy to think of his love and guidance as we eat our candy!

The "J" that the candy makes when turned upside down can stand for the name of Jesus. God has given Jesus "*the name that is above every name, that at the name of Jesus every knee should bow, in heaven and on earth and under the earth, and every tongue acknowledge that Jesus Christ is Lord, to the glory of God the Father*" (Philippians 2:9-11). This is a picture of worship. If we want joy and peace in our lives, we can find it by bowing in surrender to Jesus Christ, acknowledging that he is Lord.

The hardness of the candy is a reminder that that Jesus is the Rock. Psalm 18:2 tells us that "*The Lord is my rock, my fortress and my deliverer; my God is my rock, in whom I take refuge.*" Refuge covers a lot of territory. It is a place of shelter or protection from danger or difficulty. It's a person who gives us help or comfort. It's also a place of retreat. God is all of those things for us. What a comfort to know that our God is strong and that his strength is our refuge!

The white of the candy points to the purity of Jesus. Even though he was tempted, Christ was without sin. Hebrews 4:15 refers to Jesus as our high priest – the one who can go to the Father on our behalf. It says, "*For we do not have a high priest who is unable to empathize with our weaknesses, but we have one who has been tempted in every way just as we are – yet he did not sin.*" Because of this, we can go to him for help with our own temptations.

The candy's peppermint flavor represents the hyssop plant, a member of the mint family mentioned in Psalm 51:7. "*Cleanse me with hyssop, and I shall be clean; wash me, and I shall be whiter than snow.*" We can eat those candy J's, knowing that Jesus makes us clean. Think peppermint, hyssop, clean taste, and cleansed from sin.

The red stripes on the candy may stand for the blood Christ shed for us on the cross. "*For you know that God paid a ransom to save you…the precious blood of Christ, the sinless, spotless Lamb of God*" (1 Peter 1:18-19 NLT). We are made right with God when we believe that Jesus died for us. The red on those candy canes can bring great joy and comfort to us through our belief in Jesus as Son of God and Savior. And who does Jesus want to believe in him? All of us. All of us! It is not his will that even one of us be lost. That's what Christmas is all about.

So next time you see one of those festive sticks of sugar, remember our Shepherd, the name of Jesus, our Rock, Christ's purity, and the forgiveness of our sins though him. Maybe it's not just a candy cane any more. It's a delicious reminder of our Lord and his love for all of us.

chapter fifty-two

The Gift Exchange

My husband has given me great gifts over our five decades of marriage, but I've also received some rather unusual ones. The first year we were married, he gave me a little outdoor grill on my birthday. On another occasion his sister gave him five dollars to get me something, so he bought two decks of playing cards. One anniversary he gave me new ice trays for the freezer. We needed them, but I was hoping for something a bit more romantic. He's doing much better now. Recently, he gave me a gift certificate for rocks—not jewelry, mind you, but rocks for the front yard.

We don't always get what we're hoping for. Have you ever felt ripped off after one of those Christmas party gift exchanges? Maybe you spent more than you should have for something really special, but ended up going home with a jeweled gravy ladle (yes, those really do exist) or an old DVD of a B-grade movie.

Remember when you were in school and everyone brought a gift? The teacher put numbers on them, and everyone drew a number from a bowl. Perhaps the Yahtzee game you brought was cool, but you went home with six number two pencils. If this has been your experience, I have great news for you. You've been invited to a holy gift exchange, and you're going to come out ahead.

John 3:16 describes the trade. *"For God so loved the world that he gave his one and only Son, that whoever believes in him shall not perish but have eternal life."* Nice Exchange! We give ourselves—our old, rotten, headed-for-destruction selves—to God through our belief in him, and he gives us eternal life.

Romans 6:23 tells us, "*For the wages of sin is death, but the gift of God is eternal life through Christ Jesus our Lord.*" We get to give our sin to the one who died for it. Then we ask him for forgiveness and receive everlasting life. Wow! We trade in sin for life with him here and now and life forever after death.

Here's more good news. He's not going to change his mind and ask for his gifts back after he gets us and sees what a mess we are. "*For God's gift and His call are irrevocable. He never withdraws them once they are given, and He does not change His mind about those to whom He gives His grace or to whom He sends His call.*" (Romans 11:29 AMP). We give our inconsistent selves and receive God's permanent grace.

The Bible is full of other great gift exchanges. Isaiah 40:29 tells us that, "*He gives strength to the weary, and increases the power of the weak.*" We bring weakness and weariness and go home with strength and power.

Titus 2:14 proclaims that Christ, "*gave himself for us to redeem us from all wickedness and to purify for himself a people that are his very own, eager to do what is good.*" We bring sin, even those stinky ones that no one knows about, and go home with purity and enthusiasm to do good things because Christ gave his life.

Isaiah, Chapter 61 tells us that we get to trade:

- bad news for good tidings
- a broken heart for a healed one
- slavery for freedom
- sadness and mourning for his consolation and joy

You know, at Christmas time we have this naughty or nice thing in our heads. We tend to tell ourselves, "be good so you will get a gift. If you aren't good, you won't get a thing." This leads us to thinking that if we don't receive, we aren't good and we don't deserve anything. Please! Let's not carry that worldly thinking into the spiritual realm. It isn't true.

Ephesians 2:8 (AMP), "*For it is by free grace [God's undeserved favor to us] that you are saved through faith. And this salvation is not of yourselves [of your own doing, it came not through your own striving] but it is the gift of God.*" We can't be good enough. If we could, Christ wouldn't have had to die to save us. This gift is free.

It's very clear that we "win" the gift exchange. We draw the best number. We receive the greatest gift when we acknowledge Jesus Christ as our Savior. Why, why, why does God do this for us? Because he loves us. He died for us. He paid for us. We belong to him.

Maybe we should make a list, checking it way more than twice, of the gifts God has given us. Then we should thank him, not with just a little thank you note, but with a continuous song of praise. He brings the best gifts to the party, and we get to have them all.

chapter fifty-three

Stirring Spoons

I love to cook, and today I want to talk about an important part of cooking – stirring the pot. When you cook, if you don't stir the pot, food might stick to the bottom—not a good thing to have happen. It ruins the food and makes the pot very difficult to clean.

Sometimes you need to stir to see what's in the pot. There may be some ingredients that need to be brought up to the surface and removed. Oooops! That carrot got too brown. It must have stuck to the bottom. I'll take that out. Who put those lima beans in there? Yuck! Out they come. Too much flour. Look at those lumps! Out they come. My goodness! What's that tomato stem doing in there?

God often has to "stir our pots"—stir us—to keep us from sticking to the bottom, from sinking to our lowest level and staying there. He may allow us to be stirred to see what's in us. Hopefully, when we go through that, we can see what's in us that doesn't belong. Then we can cooperate with God to remove it.

You know what God uses as stirring spoons, don't you? He uses people and circumstances. Do you have a few stirring spoons in your life? A stirring may go like this (in your head, that is).

- "If she asks me one more time to clean the garage, I'm going to throw something." What's in that pot? Anger?
- "If he doesn't clean that garage, I'm not going to cook for a week. He'll starve." (Hmmm, is that a little revenge floating to the top?)

Here's a little monologue for you of a very stirred up woman. Try to find what's being brought up to the surface in her life.

"I'm so glad that I'm never early and never late. Jane always admires my perfect timing when I pick her up for Bible study. Now, where are those car keys? Bert always puts them where I can't find them. It's his fault if I'm late. Oh, here they are, in my purse.

"I told those kids to bring in their bikes. I'll be late now because I have to do it for them. I'm going to ground them for a week. I'll just have to drive a little over the speed limit to be on time.

"Hi, Jane. Get in the car. No, I'm not late. You must have come out early. Get in. I can't wait to tell you what's going on between John and Lucy...Well, good grief! You stupid, careless driver! She didn't stop at that stop sign! Look at her putting on her makeup while she drives... and look at him on his cell phone, thinks he's so important. Humph! Anyway, John told Lucy --- WOW! That guy must be going 90. Where's a cop when you need one? Think of all the revenue our state could get if the cops would just do their job. 'Probably off drinking coffee and eating doughnuts. Well, if we just had a good governor, things would be different. Man! Politicians! Lazy bunch of no good...I hate that guy on the city council, you know the one who...

"For heaven's sake! That kid almost hit us. Look at that fancy car he's driving. 'Wonder where he got the money for that? 'Bet he sells drugs. Probably uses them too. I'm so glad that I'm not addicted to anything. By the way, did you go to the Weight Watchers' meeting last night? The reason I wasn't there is Bert wanted to try that all-you-can-eat buffet on Cypress Parkway. Anyway, if that kid isn't selling drugs, his parents bought him the car. Spoiled rotten! Young people today have no sense of the value of a dollar. See that Starbuck's over there. Those kids go in there and pay as much for one cup of coffee as I pay for a whole pound. I went in there once. What a snooty clerk! 'Acted like I should know what a karma, marma, mocha latte is. I was so offended by her attitude. Well, we're here now. I'll tell you about John and Lucy later. It's awful."

Stir. Stir. Stir! What came to the surface here? Impatience, judgmental attitude, meanness, self-righteousness, pride, covetousness, anger, hatred, gossiping, and I'm sure I missed a few. What can we do when things like that are brought out in us? We surely don't want them stuck in us or hidden in us. 1 Thessalonians 5:18 says, "*Give thanks in all circumstances,*" so we can start there.

- Thank God for the opportunity to get rid of a wrong reaction to an irritating situation.
- Thank God for the person or the situation that showed us the reaction.
- Ask God to bless the person.

Romans 8:28-29 tells us, "*We know that in all things God works for the good of those who love him, who have been called according to his purpose. For those God foreknew he also predestined to be conformed to the image of his Son.*" We can't become like him without our stirring spoons, without those people and circumstances that help us remove anything that interferes with the molding process. Here are four steps that can help.

1. Give the reaction to Jesus. You name it, hatred, self-righteousness, pride...whatever. There's no need to disguise it or analyze it. Just acknowledge that Jesus died for that sin.
2. Repent, be truly sorry, and desire to change.
3. Ask God to fill the empty space left by getting rid of what the stirring spoon revealed. Ask him to fill that space with the fruit of the Holy Spirit.
4. Thank him for doing it.

If we keep at this process, we become what the Bible calls overcomers. We can let God fill us with the fruit of the Spirit—love, joy, peace, patience, kindness, goodness, faithfulness, gentleness, and self-control. Now, my friends, that's a terrific fruit salad, a dish fit for our King.

This week when a stirring spoon comes along, let's follow the steps and rejoice that we aren't sticking to the bottom of the pot. We're getting rid of a lot of junk. God is working on us for our good, and that's worth the stirring.

chapter fifty-four

Continue Stirring

L ast week, we talked about stirring spoons and how we sometimes stir what we cook to see what's in the pot. In much the same way, God uses people and situations to stir us up, to reveal reactions in us that need to be removed. When a driver cuts us off in traffic, some of us get so angry we scream at him even though he's long gone. That's a stirring spoon, a situation used by God to reveal anger in us. Here's a quick review of how we are to handle reactions like anger, stress, hatred, meanness, worry, and whatever else might stir us up.

- Thank God for showing us what he wants to get out of us.
- Thank God for the person or situation that stirred us.
- Ask God to bless the stirrer.
- Give the reaction to Christ by naming the sin. Remember, he died for that sin.
- Repent. Be truly sorry and willing to change.
- Ask God to replace what you have given to him with more of himself and the fruit of the Holy Spirit. (Love, joy, patience, kindness, goodness, faithfulness, gentleness, and self-control)

Did you meet up with a stirring spoon this week? Were you able to do a few of these steps? Hard, isn't it? Perhaps it's hard to admit to God that we have anything wrong within us, because we have a misconception about God. We may believe that if we admit there's something "bad" in us, God will disown us or forsake us. We may think that our worth to God is based on being good, or on not having any defects.

Good News! In God's eyes, our worth as a person isn't reduced by our faults and our failures. We are of value because we belong to him. Because of Jesus' work on the cross, God accepts us just as we are, even though we aren't what he wants us to be...yet. Listen, we don't have to have the Good Housekeeping seal of approval. We have God's approval through his Son.

Another reason we're afraid to look at our flaws and weaknesses could be that we received unloving discipline as we grew up. We might have been treated in a harsh or an unloving way. So, when the stirring spoon shows us something that needs discipline, we immediately think a tyrant with a stick is going to beat us, or a mean spirited God is going to clobber us with cruel words. Thinking that God will deal with us in that way will keep us from self-discovery. We'll resist knowing ourselves, and we'll hide at the bottom of the pot.

I grew up with my mom, dad, and big sister. Two girls, no brother. One girl was pretty and popular and found lots of favor with many people. The other was an overweight tomboy. Can you guess which one I was? I was the one who needed plenty of discipline. I was never beaten, but the sad thing, the thing that has been tough for me in my spiritual life, was a phrase said over and over again to me when I came up short, "Aren't you ashamed of yourself?" Shame can keep us from examining our hearts until we know God loves us. Anger can do it. Fear? Jealousy? What's your blockage?

"*Because of the Lord's great love we are not consumed, for his compassions never fail*" (Lamentations 3:22). God is not against us for our sins. He is for us against our sins. We must learn to embrace God's loves for us. We won't like seeing our flaws, but with his help and his forgiveness we can overcome them. Then we must forgive ourselves as he forgives us.

Let's not be afraid to say, as the Psalmist did in Psalm 139:23-24, "*Search me, God, and know my heart; test me and know my anxious thoughts. See if there is any offensive way in me, and lead me in the way everlasting.*"

Next time you look into a mirror, let it remind you to examine your reactions and to submit them to Christ. Let's allow every mirror to remind us that God wants to show us things that keep us from having a close relationship with him. We can look at our sins without fear, because we can repent of them and give them to God. We will be forgiven, and he will change us.

Let's proclaim to God, "We trust you! We know you love us! Only you can change us, and we submit ourselves to you to be changed. Yes, Lord, bring on the stirring spoons. Clean us up, Lord, and mold us into your image."

chapter fifty-five

Like a Yo-yo

I once found a bag of yo-yos on sale for a remarkably low price. Guess why. Because they didn't work, not at all. I bought them anyway and gave them to some of my friends as a reminder that a "Yo-yo Life" doesn't work either.

We all have the yo-yo syndrome going on in us. We feel good, then bad; happy, then depressed; fearless, then afraid; loving, then hateful; confident, then anxious. We're like that because we're human. Unfortunately, and I'm speaking from experience here, we often react to these ups and downs by doing what one old song title says, "Looking for Love in All the Wrong Places." Most of those places involve some kind of sensual pleasure, anything to satisfy our senses. We turn to alcohol or drugs. We want to numb our feelings.

We need a lift. We need to get that yo-yo up. Maybe we drink too much coffee. We might overeat, comforting ourselves with food. My personal favorite artificial high is the sugar high. Or maybe we go shopping. And, gentlemen, you are not exempt. Women may get a kick from a new pair of shoes, but many of you guys buy new electronics with a bigger price tag. Both highs disappear when the bills arrive.

We can numb our pain in plenty of other ways. We might become completely absorbed in television. Do we know more about who gets kicked off *Dancing with the Stars* than we do about Christ? Maybe our lift comes from making it to the next level of a computer game. "Hey! I got the highest score." Guess what? Someone else will get a higher one.

It doesn't last. None of these lifts or highs last or satisfy us. We all go down again. The ups and downs of life are a part of reality. So, what are we to do? In order to be grounded in reality we need to be grounded in Christ. We must trust him with everything. Often, when we are down, we say to ourselves, "Well, I guess I just need to try harder." Ah, but it's the trusting, not the trying, that does the trick. Proverbs 3:5-6 says, "*Trust in the Lord with all your heart and lean not on your own understanding; in all your ways submit to him, and he will direct your paths.*" The God who saves us by his grace is also powerful enough to sustain us and to keep us steady—steady, not yo-yoing up and down.

The Bible is full of stories of God's yo-yo people. They obeyed God until things were good (up), then turned away (down). Later they would return to worshipping him (up). Then they would worship idols (down). Psalm 78:37 (AMP) says: "*Their hearts were not right or sincere with Him, neither were they faithful and steadfast to His Covenant.*"

Are we any more steadfast than they? Probably not, but there's hope for us anyway. "*If we confess our sins, he is faithful and just and will forgive us our sins and purify us from all unrighteousness*" (1 John 1:9). Romans 11:29 (AMP) tells us that God "*does not change His mind about those to whom He gives His grace or to whom He sends His call.*" Yea! God does not yo-yo! He doesn't love us one minute and not the next. He doesn't call us to belong to him then, when he sees what yo-yo's we are, decide to cast us away. God is always steadfast. His Word is always trustworthy. God and his Word, these are our only hope for relief from the yo-yo syndrome.

We know what to do mentally and spiritually. Trust him. What else can we do to exhibit our steadfastness? Paul wrote, "*Be earnest and unwearied and steadfast in your prayer life, being both alert and intent in your praying with thanksgiving*" (Colossians 4:2 AMP). Hmmmm! Pray, not once in a while, not just when we're needy, but steadfastly. That's something we can do.

Paul also wrote, "*So, my dear brothers and sisters, be strong and immovable. Always work enthusiastically for the Lord, for you know that nothing you do for the Lord is ever useless*" (1 Corinthians 15:58 NLT). Has God directly or through his Word told us something we should do (or not do)? Let's jump on it. Let's be quick to obey. "*We are God's handiwork, created in Christ Jesus to do good works, which God prepared in advance for us to do*" (Ephesians 2:10). God has prepared us and made us able to do the work he desires us to do.

Isn't it great that God can change us and use us as he himself breaks that yo-yo mess? We'll never be perfectly steadfast this side of heaven. But the next time we feel ourselves "unwound," or dropping to the bottom, let's say what Psalm 42:5 says, *"Why, my soul, are you downcast? Why so disturbed within me? Put your hope in God, for I will yet praise him, my Savior and my God."*

chapter fifty-six

A Tangled Mess

When I sew, which is not often, I hate it when my thread tangles up between the cloth and the needle. Most of the time, I just have to cut it, take out several stitches, re-thread the needle, and start over. Frustrating. Have you ever been fishing and gotten your line tangled around an underwater tree branch? All you can do is cut the line, losing the hook, bait, and bobber.

Once, when I was about six years old, I went to the movies with my cousin Norma, who was eight. Norma was chewing a big wad of bubble gum. She was tired of chewing it and couldn't figure how to get rid of it, so she stuck it in my hair. Now, that was the worst of all tangles. I had very short hair for a while.

Sometimes our lives are tangled messes. We get knotted up and tangled with sin in our lives. "What sin?" you may ask. The sin of worry, of neglecting our Lord Jesus, of gluttony, of lust, or selfishness…We're easily drawn into the trap of sin. Look at these verses: "*For the Lord sees clearly what a man does, examining every path he takes. An evil man is held captive by his own sins; they are ropes that catch and hold him*" (Proverbs 5:21-22 NLT). Ever feel trapped like that? I do. If you could look at me today, I'm sure you'd see some rope.

The more we lapse into sinful behavior, the more lies we tell to cover it up, or the more we listen to Satan's lies about our situation. Isaiah 5:18 (NLT) warns, "*What sorrow for those who drag their sins behind them with ropes made of lies.*" What sins are we denying or excusing? How exhausted are we with dragging around our sins? How can we cut those ropes? The answer to all those questions is to ask God to show us our sins, to confess them to him, and to let him forgive us.

"Fear of man will prove to be a snare, but whoever trusts in the Lord is kept safe" (Proverbs 29:25). Fearing people is a dangerous trap. We don't do or say what God wants us to, because we're afraid of what people will think. Yet the Bible says we must obey God rather than man. While it's kind of depressing and sad to see ourselves tangled up or trapped in sin, there's good news. The Lord has said that he will rescue us from every trap and become our place of safety. He will comfort us and free us.

Did you get all of that? Jesus is our way to freedom from all the tangled messes in our lives.

- Are we trapped by bad news all around us? He brings good news. (You can read all the good news in the Bible.)
- Are we sad, depressed or brokenhearted? He brings us comfort and a way out.
- Are we being held captive by anything—poverty or ill health, anger, lust, or selfishness? He offers us release. No prison can hold us if he frees us. According to the Bible in John 8:36, if we choose Jesus as our Lord and Savior, he will set us free and we will be "free indeed."

Don't let me leave you with the idea that making the choice to follow Christ ends all problems. It does end the question of where we will spend eternity and the question of what to do about sin in our lives. However, we'll all have heartaches and difficulties until we die, because we live in a fallen world with human beings, and we are human. But choosing God means we are never alone in our difficulties. He'll give us his power to endure and to overcome them. They won't hold us captive. With Jesus Christ in us, we know that everything is going to be okay, even if the "okay" scenario isn't the one we would choose.

We are a bit like my sewing threads, often twisted and tangled, or even broken. God is the only one who can untangle us and set us free. Hebrews 12:1 tells us to, *"Throw off everything that hinders and the sin that so easily entangles."* Each of us needs to untangle the main thread of our lives, the connection between us and God. We can only do that by his power. Once we give ourselves to him, all the other tangles and snarls can be undone. Our lives don't have to be a tangled mess.

chapter fifty-seven

Tongue Suppressors

Nutrition books, vitamin ads, news articles on the latest diets, they're all so confusing. Eat mostly protein. No, load up on carbs. Don't eat sugar. Eat anything you want as long as you take the right pills. No fat, low fat, just use olive oil. I wonder if everyone has spent as much time and money as I have on learning what should go into my mouth. Of course, what we eat is important, but the world is so preoccupied with food that it even says, "You are what you eat."

Want to know what Jesus said?

"Listen and understand. What goes into someone's mouth does not defile them, but what comes out of their mouth, that is what defiles them" (Matthew 15:10-11). We might disagree about what should go into our mouths, but God has been clear in his Word about what should come out of it. What we say is important.

When I go to the doctor, he takes a fat stick—a tongue suppressor—and puts it on my tongue to keep it from moving while he takes a look around. Do you sometimes wish your tongue would be still on its own and not get you into so much trouble? I do! Our tongues are important to God.

- *"Come, my children, listen to me; I will teach you the fear of the Lord. Whoever of you loves life and desires to see many good days, keep your tongue from evil and your lips from telling lies"* (Psalm 34:11-13).

- *"Those who guard their lips preserve their lives, but those who speak rashly will come to ruin"* (Proverbs 13:3). In other words, if you want to stay out of trouble, keep your mouth shut.
- *"The tongue has the power of life and death"* (Proverbs 18:21).

We especially need to guard our mouths when we're going through any kind of difficulty. It's so easy to let troubles—job loss, illness, a wayward child, any sort of crisis—make us angry, or bitter, or short tempered, or tired, so that we say things we don't want to say. We dish out death instead of life.

Before there were so many lab tests available, doctors used to say, "How are you?" You'd try to tell them. Then, they'd say, "Let me see your tongue." They could tell a lot just by looking at your tongue.

What if God said, "How's your spiritual life going?" Then he might say, "Let me see your tongue. When I've seen your tongue, I'll know the condition of your heart." Matthew 12:34 says, *"For the mouth speaks what the heart is full of."*) There are many diseases of the tongue. We all suffer from them now and then. Here are just a few:

Excessive Talking. Proverbs 10:19 (GNT) warns that, *"The more you talk, the more likely you are to sin. If you are wise, you will keep quiet."* James calls the tongue a restless evil. People who run on and on, breathing in the middle of a sentence, using "and" or "so" instead of a period, often have restless hearts. They need peace.

Idleworditis. *"You can be sure that on the Judgement Day you will have to give account of every useless word you have ever spoken"* (Matthew 12:36 GNT). Please don't get in line behind me on Judgment Day. If you do, you'll have a long wait, because I have many idle words for which I must account. If we could follow Matthew 5:37, we could eliminate lots of careless or idle words. *"All you need to say is simply 'Yes' or 'No'; anything beyond this comes from the evil one."*

Gossip. Thumper, the rabbit from the Walt Disney movie *Bambi*, said his mother taught him, "If you can't say anything nice, don't say anything at all." We'd have a quiet world if we all followed that advice. Psalm 15:1-3 says much the same thing, encouraging us to refrain from speaking slander or hurting others with our words.

Lying. *"The Lord detests lying lips, but he delights in people who are trust-worthy"* (Proverbs 12:22). That's pretty clear! Lying isn't a matter of perspective, either. Revelation 21:8 puts liars on equal status with cowards, unbelievers, the vile, murderers, the sexually immoral, those who practice magic arts, and idolaters. Lying is a serious disease. Of course, there are many others like flattery (using words as a way to get something from someone) and negativism (always finding something wrong with everything) and cynicism (believing the worst about every situation). James says no man can tame the tongue. Are we hopelessly diseased? Can't we do anything to be healed, maybe take some medicine or something? Yes! Here are the steps we can take to cure all these diseases of the tongue.

- First we must call our disease what it really is. It's sin.
- Then we confess it to God and receive his forgiveness.
- After that, we refuse to yield to sin again. Sure, we'll have the thoughts, but we can resist the temptation to say them.

If we take those steps, the time period between the outbreaks of our tongue disease will lengthen. We keep on. We learn to say what God says. At some point, we'll realize that our mouths are not giving us as much trouble as they once did. So don't despair. We're curable. And every time we use our words for good (to bless others, to praise God, to show love, patience, goodness, and kindness) our disease reduces. We're getting healed. Praise God!

Let me share some practical things I've learned over the last forty years in my own life. These will help prevent "outbreak of tongue" problems.

- Sometimes the best rule is simply, "Bite your tongue" (especially if you have a teenager). We're better off if we don't say all that we want to say.
- Just because something is true doesn't mean we have to say it. It's best to use wisdom and love.
- Not every word that comes into our minds has to come out of our mouths. We can think something hurtful and let it go. Once we put the words out there, we can't get them back.

175

- There's enough pain in the world, enough discouragement, and enough of every kind of hurt. No more needs to come from us, out of our mouths.

What comes out of our mouths is far more important than what goes into them. Psalm 141:3 gives us just the prayer we need. "*Set a guard over my mouth, Lord; keep watch over the door of my lips.*" Amen and amen!

chapter fifty-eight

Trust

One Sunday, a mom struggled in church with her wiggly young son. He just wouldn't stay seated. He kept standing up, even after his mother repeatedly told him to sit down. Finally, she had to warn him that he'd get a spanking after church if he refused to sit. He did sit, but with a scowl on his face and his arms folded across his chest, he said, "I may be sitting down on the outside, but on the inside I am still standing."[21] Circumstances make us feel as if we are down, but today I want to tell you about something that will keep you standing up on the inside, the trust we place in God.

When was the last time you had a Tootsie Pop? Remember how hard it was to eat it slowly? We were all in a hurry to get to the center, to that chewy, chocolate treat. The good stuff. Well, the good stuff in the center of our spirits can be a deep, steady trust in God. He wants that for us. First, though, let's establish from God's Word the places where we shouldn't put our trust.

"*Blessed is the one who trusts in the Lord, who does not look to the proud, to those who turn aside to false gods*" (Psalm 40:4). Here's what that might look like in today's terms. We ought not to put our trust in:

- That new computer system. "That great technology will do magical things for us." Really?
- Our many college degrees. "The more I know the better off I'll be. I'm smart enough to do anything." Well, maybe not.
- Money, riches. "As soon as we have enough money all will be well. We won't need God. We'll know how to get ev-

erything." Of course, money can't save us from our sins, keep us healthy, or give us wisdom.

"*It is better to take refuge in the Lord than to trust in humans. It is better to take refuge in the Lord than to trust in princes*" (Psalm 118:8-9). No matter how powerful a man is, he's not where we place our trust. No matter how good, kind, Christian or loving a man is, he's not where we place our trust. Our trust belongs in God. My daddy's favorite hymn puts it this way, "I dare not trust the sweetest frame, but wholly lean on Jesus' name."[22]

"*Some trust in chariots and some in horses, but we trust in the name of the Lord our God*" (Psalm 20:7). I guess a new BMW or Jaguar, no matter the horsepower, won't do much for us! Some versions of the Bible relate chariots and horses to weapons. So we can't trust in those either.

Now, this next example is a doozy. We are not to place our trust in ourselves and in what we do, not even in our good deeds or what we do for God. Jesus was getting ready to tell a parable. The Bible says he "*told this story to some who had great confidence in their own righteousness and scorned everyone else*" (Luke 18:9 NLT). Then it relates the parable of the Pharisee, or religious man, and the tax collector.

The Pharisee listed all his good religious works. I never cheat. I don't sin. I don't commit adultery. I fast twice a week. I give a tenth of all my income to God. Jesus explained that this man, so proud of his goodness, would not be justified before God. So, obviously, our core trust must not be in our sweet, good, religious selves. It must be in God alone. And trusting God alone brings great advantages. God promises to help those who trust him. He says those who trust him will never be abandoned or forsaken. He offers strength and joy and blessing to those who lean on him. We're even told that "*unfailing love surrounds those who trust the Lord*" (Psalm 32:10).

Okay. I'm sold. Are you? Now we need to figure out practical ways to start trusting God and then to keep on trusting him. We can start by letting our testing time be our trusting time. When things are hard (and we all experience trouble to some degree and in some way), see those times as an opportunity to trust. The Apostle Paul wrote that the troubles he and those with him had suffered were to keep them from relying on themselves and to make them rely only on God. When Jesus was insulted, he didn't retaliate. When he suffered, he didn't threaten to get even. He trusted himself to God. Hard times are opportunities to trust God.

Look to the Word of God. Proverbs 3:5-7 contains some very specific dos and don'ts about how to trust.

- Do trust the Lord completely and consistently, not as a last resort.
- Don't depend on your own understanding. Don't be impressed with your own wisdom.
- Do seek his will for your path. Let God direct you.
- Don't mess around with evil.

There's nothing vague in that list, and nothing we can't get started on right away. Reading the Bible isn't enough. We're meant to investigate it, to try it for ourselves, to believe it, and to act on the things the Lord says. The best way to do that is to look into the Bible on our own. Then we're not taking someone else's word about a subject. We're taking God's Word about it.

There's an old hymn that means a lot to me. It stresses that trust comes by taking Jesus at his Word. The most important line to me is this one, "How I've proved him (Jesus) o'er and o'er!" The longer we trust him, and the more times we experience his faithfulness, the stronger our trust grows.

The last line of the chorus says, "Jesus, Jesus, Precious Jesus. Oh for grace to trust him more." We acknowledge that God's grace allows us to trust. If we've accepted Christ as Savior, we have that grace. We already have it, so we are without excuse. We can trust God. We'll never do it perfectly this side of heaven, but we can do it. Here's more of that wonderful hymn.

> 'Tis so sweet to trust in Jesus, and to take Him at His word.
> Just to rest upon His promise, and to know, "Thus saith the Lord."
> Jesus, Jesus, how I trust Him! How I've proved Him o'er and o'er!
> Jesus. Jesus, precious Jesus, O for grace to trust Him more![23]

That's our prayer for the week. We ask for grace to trust him now and forever. It's what's deep inside that counts, our trust in God.

chapter fifty-nine

Two Cents Worth

W hen I see a couple of pennies on the street, I pick them up. One study I read reported that about three-fourths of us do that, but nearly half of us think our mint should just stop making those nearly worthless coins. Today, you'll get my two cents on something. That's supposed to mean it will be short, but, well, you know me. Our topic is that of giving in the right spirit, and the best way to start is with a passage from Mark 12:41-44 (NLT).

> *"Jesus sat down near the collection box in the Temple and watched as the crowds dropped in their money. Many rich people put in large amounts. Then a poor widow came and dropped in two small coins. Jesus called his disciples to him and said, 'I tell you the truth, this poor widow has given more than all the others who are making contributions. For they gave a tiny part of their surplus, but she, poor as she is, has given everything she had to live on.'"*

Preachers sometimes like to use this scripture to encourage sacrificial giving when the church finances get low. That's not what I want to emphasize today. I think we should look at what Jesus said shortly before the scene at the treasury. Just a few verses earlier, in Mark 12:29-30, Jesus was asked to describe the most important commandments. He answered, *"Love the Lord your God with all your heart and with all your soul and with all your mind and with all your strength."* He went on to say, *"Love your neighbor as yourself. There is no commandment greater than these."* So we might consider this: Jesus knew the widow gave more than all the others, because she gave out of the spirit and motive of love. Any time we give anything, it should be with love. Jesus was looking at how people were giving, not what they were giving.

In verse 38-40 of this same chapter, Jesus warned his disciples to,

"Watch out for the teachers of the law. They like to walk around in flowing robes and be greeted with respect in the marketplaces, and have the most important seats in the synagogues and the places of honor at banquets. They devour widows' houses and for a show (to cover up their deeds) they make lengthy prayers. These men will be punished most severely."

In the very next scene of Chapter 12, we observe the rich people and the widow contributing to the temple coffers. Perhaps like lengthy, showy prayers, the rich also made large contributions to cover up what sort of people they really were and to draw attention away from their ungodly deeds. *The Amplified Bible* puts it this way, *"Many rich people were throwing in large sums."* Can't you imagine the grand physical movement of their giving, a show to draw attention? Maybe the throwing of coins even made a noise to get attention. But the Bible says the widow put her gift in with no show or attention, quietly, generously and (in my opinion) happily. She didn't have to give her all out of some sort of obligation. She wanted to give it.

Suppose the widow, seeing these wealthy givers and the large amounts being given, had thought, "Well, what am I doing? These two tiny coins won't matter at all. I want to give. I love God, but certainly what I am able to give won't make any difference. I'll be embarrassed to go up there with such a piddling sum. I just won't bother to do this." Does that attitude ring a bell for any of you? It does for me, because I've done that. In my mind, the words go like this:

- I'd offer to help, but I have only an hour a week to give. They'll get somebody who has more time.
- I could plan that program or cook for that meeting. I know how, but I'm not a professional. They'll get someone who can do it much better than I.

- I'd be happy to lead that small Bible study, but I'm sure they can get someone much more knowledgeable than I.
- I love to sing, but I'm no soloist and I don't read music too well. They'll get someone with much more talent than I for the choir.
- I feel really sorry for the hard time that family has had. I'd call, but what could I say? Someone who has counseling skills should do it.

How many times have I missed God's best because I wouldn't give or do the little things within my abilities? Just think. If the widow had left the synagogue without giving her two coins, we wouldn't have this scene in the Bible or this teaching by Jesus in this chapter of Mark. Why, she's famous! Two little coins—recorded for all the ages.

What little gifts do we have that we haven't given to God's kingdom? Remember that Jesus fed 5,000 people with five loaves and two fish. Wow! What might he do with our little gifts and talents and time? Everything we give him out of love, he multiplies for his use and for our certain good.

This week, if you come across a penny, whether on the street or elsewhere, I hope it will cause you to remember two things:

- We are to give because we love God and others, not for show or reward.
- Nothing we give or do for his kingdom is too small for God to use. Don't discount your "little things." God will make them big.

And that's my two cents on the subject.

chapter sixty

What Are You Looking At?

T he world gives us plenty of well-meaning advice about where to look, where to focus our attention.

- "Looking ahead will keep you from falling behind."
- "Keep your eyes on the prize."
- "Seeing is believing."

All of these sayings have nuggets of truth in them, but which of them will really help us?

"Looking ahead will keep you from falling behind." Jesus said, "*No one who puts a hand to the plow and looks back is fit for service in the kingdom of God*" (Luke 9:62). Any farmer can tell you what will happen if you look back while plowing. You will get very crooked rows. Are we spending lots of time thinking about our pasts? If we are, I wonder if we're thinking about the good things behind us. Probably not. More likely, we're nursing and rehearsing the "bad stuff" that's happened to us or the "bad stuff" we've done. But God forgives our sins, takes us through the hard times, and offers us a fresh start every day. Psalm 77:11-12 describes a much better way to look back at our lives. "*I will remember the deeds of the Lord; yes, I will remember your miracles of long ago. I will consider all your works and meditate on all your mighty deeds.*" That's the good kind of looking back!

"Keep your eyes on the prize." If we have become followers of God, we need to spend time looking forward to the prize that awaits us. I often use the term "looking forward." I'm looking forward to Christmas, a good movie, eating lunch with a friend, or maybe taking a nap. In Titus

2:12-13, we learn that we're to live lives of wisdom and devotion to God while we look forward to the day when we'll see Jesus, our Savior.

Nobody's present situation is perfect. Should we describe all the parts of our lives that are wrong, hard or ugly for us right now? Oh, no, we should not. In 2 Corinthians 4, we are instructed not to look at the trouble we can see. Instead we are to fix our eyes on, or give our attention to, that which cannot be seen. What we see now will soon be gone. It's temporary. God. Love. Peace. Joy. Those will last forever, and so will eternal life through Christ's payment for our sins when he died on the cross.

That brings us to the phrase, "Seeing is believing." That's not always true. Believing is seeing, as backwards as that sounds. Sometimes we have to believe before we see. That's faith. How can we hold on to our faith when we can't see it? By reading and believing God's Word. I can almost hear you saying, "There you go again, Beth, making it sound easier than it is." Believe me, at my age, I know how the world, the flesh, and the devil keep us from reading the Bible and from prayer. The longer we seek God, though, the more easily we recognize the traps and circumstances that cause us to do everything else except seek God. Let's just get over ourselves and do it. Come on! We can fight the good fight of faith. We can read the Bible and pray and look to our Lord in times of trouble.

God makes it very clear in his Word that where we focus our attention is important. Where should we be looking? Here's a sampling of God's answer to that question.

"My eyes are ever on the Lord, for only he will release my feet from the snare."
—Psalm 25:15

"My eyes are fixed on you, Sovereign Lord; in you I take refuge."
—Psalm 141:8

While our eyes are on the Lord, his eyes are on us. He doesn't look away. He doesn't forget us.

"The eyes of the Lord are on those who fear him, on those whose hope is in his unfailing love."

—Psalm 33:18

"The eyes of the Lord are on the righteous and his ears are attentive to their prayer."

—1 Peter 3:12

Does "righteous" mean that we're watched and heard only when we do everything right? No, not at all. We receive our righteousness by accepting and acknowledging the payment that Jesus made for us when he died for us on the cross. So let me ask you one more time, "What are we looking at?" Is our attention fixed on our past, our present, and our future, or are we focused on our God—our Help and Friend and only hope.

The word "behold" means to hold in view or to fix our gaze on, to give our attention to. With that in mind, consider this verse, Revelation 3:20 (NASB). *"Behold,* (Look. Keep what I'm about to say in your gaze. Pay attention now.) *I stand at the door and knock; if anyone hears My voice and opens the door, I will come in to him and will dine with him, and he with Me."* Isn't that the perfect instruction for where we should look? We look at him, we behold him, our Lord and our God.

So, what are you looking at?

chapter sixty-one

Whatcha Got?

I'd like to tell you a story. It comes from the book of Mark, chapter six, but I'll be inserting a bit of my own perspective.

Jesus sent his disciples two by two on a road trip. It was a mission trip, really. He gave them authority over demons and a set of unusual instructions. A walking staff was all they could take with them—no extra clothes, shoes, or food, and no moneybag. Not a luxury outing, was it? But they did a great job! They preached the gospel, encouraged people to repent of their sins, drove out demons, and anointed many with oil. They had the joy of seeing people healed. I can imagine they came home very happy, but tired.

Upon returning, they got the news about John the Baptist. He'd been beheaded by Herod. Now the disciples were tired, shocked, and sad. As the disciples gave Jesus the reports of their trips, the crowds continued to come and go and press in to see Jesus. The disciples were kept so busy that (according to the Bible) they didn't even have time to eat. They were tired, happy/sad, and hungry.

Jesus saw the disciples' physical and emotional condition and said to them, "*Come with me by yourselves to a quiet place and get some rest*" (Mark 6:31). They got into a boat and headed to a place of solitude. I imagine the disciples were feeling relieved, looking forward to a getaway. But the crowds figured out where they were going and ran on ahead, arriving at the retreat to greet the boat.

The Bible says that when Jesus saw the people, "*He had compassion on them, because they were like sheep without a shepherd*" (v. 34). Now, how do you suppose the disciples were feeling? They weren't going to have a rest after all. Another hope dashed. They were now tired, sad, hungry, disappointed, and maybe even put out with Jesus for placing the needs of all these people ahead of the needs of his own committed disciples.

Suppertime came. The disciples weren't just tired, they were exhausted, and they were surrounded by people in need. They said to Jesus, "Lord, it's late. It's getting dark. These people are hungry. Send them off into the villages to buy their dinner."

His answer was the last straw for these disciples. Jesus said, "You give them something to eat."

What? Now, exhausted, sad, hungry, disappointed, peeved, maybe even angry, I bet they thought, "After everything else, does Jesus want us to walk all the way to the villages to get food? We don't have any money. He wouldn't even let us take a moneybag for offerings on the road trip. This is over the top." They knew Jesus could do miracles, but they were in no physical or emotional state to remember such a thing. (Isn't that true of us at times?) The disciples answered Jesus by saying, "Lord, we have nothing to give. It would cost a small fortune to feed all these people."

At that point, Jesus asked them an important question and gave them a command. The question Jesus asked was, "What do you have?" The command was, "Go and see." He asks us the same question and tells us to do the same thing. We all need to take an inventory of what we have. Let's see, we have God's love, his forgiveness, his grace, his mercy, health, family, talents, strengths, abilities – all from God. In a way, finding the answer to the question, "What do you have?" could be called counting your blessings.

The disciples found that they had five loaves and two fish, and brought them to Jesus. Jesus multiplied them and fed all the people. We need to bring what we have to Jesus, especially when we're tired, sad, hungry, disappointed, peeved, angry, financially strapped, full of questions, or having doubts. You know the feeling. Even at our lowest, we must stop and hear Jesus ask, "What do you have?" We can almost hear him saying, "Go and see."

No matter how small what we have may seem to be, when we give it to Jesus he takes what is little and makes it into much. Every little thing about us is important to God. He knows our physical and emotional limitations, but he loves us. He will use, in a marvelous way, whatever we give him for his kingdom and our good.

It's time for us to remember that God can multiply our little loaves and fish—our love, talents, money, and time—when we put them in his hands. Jesus asks each of us, "What do you have? Go and see."

chapter sixty-two

Nip It in the Bud

Several years ago, I came across a book by Dr. Dennis Swanberg, a minister who is full of wit and wisdom. The description on the cover of the book said, "Humorous stories that nourish the heart." My heart can always use more nourishment, and I'll bet yours can too, so let me share one of his stories with you.

One Sunday morning, when Dennis was a kid of six or seven, he went to church and sat, as usual, in the back with some other children. His parents were seated near the front. The pastor asked, dramatically, "What shall we do with sin?"

Not knowing that the preacher was asking a rhetorical question (or even what a rhetorical question was), Dennis looked around, thinking, "Why isn't anyone answering him?" When no one volunteered to help the preacher, Dennis stood up, shrugged, and mouthed the words, "We don't know."

The preacher didn't notice the little guy. He probably couldn't even see him. Sure enough, later in his sermon, the preacher again asked, "What shall we do with sin?"

Dennis felt so sorry for the preacher that he stood up and motioned silently, "We don't know. I don't know. You don't know. Only God knows. Don't ask us, ask him."

Eventually, the preacher asked the question one last time, seriously, slowly, and dramatically, "What shall we do with sin?"

Little Dennis couldn't take it anymore. He jumped to his feet and climbed up on the pew. Inspired by a phrase made famous by Barney Fife of the old Andy Griffith Show, he yelled, "Nip it in the bud! You gotta nip it in the bud!"[24]

You know what? Little Dennis was right. I've lived long enough to learn the hard way that sin

- starts as a thought,
- grows into an imagination,
- and can then become a stronghold.

The "bud" stage is when it's just a thought. We need to stop sin there before it can move on to an imagination. We know what imagination is. We roll the idea over in our minds, thinking what it would be like to commit that sin. (We're probably wondering if we would get caught, or asking ourselves if it's really wrong, or convincing ourselves that lots of other people do it.) If we imagine it enough, we're likely to go on and do whatever we've been contemplating. If we continue in that sin, it becomes a stronghold in our lives. A stronghold is a place in us that we guard. We fortify it against God's intrusion.

Many scriptures help us "nip sin in the bud." In school we learned about the "Three R's." Today, you'll get "Five R's," the Five R's of nipping sin before it gets out of the bud stage. Here comes sin. What shall we do with it?

- Recognize the sin. We're sinners. We can't deny that fact. *"For all have sinned and fall short of the glory of God"* (Romans 3:23).
- Repent of the sin. That means that we turn away from it. We fight sin because the Bible tells us to. It also tells us we have the power to win. *"Repent, then, and turn to God, so that your sins may be wiped out,* (I love that phrase "wiped out") *that times of refreshing may come from the Lord"* (Acts 3:29).
- Receive God's forgiveness. *"Then I acknowledged my sin to you and did not cover up my iniquity. I said, 'I will confess my transgressions to the Lord.' And you forgave the guilt of my sin"* (Psalm 32:5).
- Reckon (or regard or consider) ourselves dead to the sin. In the south we say, "I reckon I can do that." Or, if asked a

question, we might answer, "I reckon so." Look at Romans 6:11-14 (NLT). *"So you also should consider yourselves to be dead to the power of sin and alive to God through Christ Jesus. Do not let sin control the way you live; do not give in to sinful desires. Do not let any part of your body become an instrument of evil to serve sin. Instead, give yourselves completely to God, for you were dead, but now you have new life. So use your whole body as an instrument to do what is right for the glory of God. Sin is no longer your master, for you no longer live under the requirements of the law. Instead, you live under the freedom of God's grace."*

- Rejoice that we are not slaves to sin and we will win the battle. *"For every child of God defeats this evil world, and we achieve this victory through our faith. And who can win this battle against the world? Only those who believe that Jesus is the Son of God."* (1 John 5:4-5 NLT)

An old Indian proverb says, "The best place to kill a cobra is in the egg." The best place to kill a sin in our lives is in our thought life. So I'll ask you, as the dramatic preacher did many years ago, "What shall we do with sin?"

Your answer? "Nip it in the bud!"

chapter sixty-three

Write it Down

I love the old song, "Count Your Blessings."[25] The lyrics tell us to, "name them one by one" in order to see what God has done. It's so important to remember our blessings and to be quick to thank God for them. When I absolutely must remember something, I write it down. Perhaps it's time to start writing down our blessings as well. Many of us already make lists for ourselves, lists of appointments, things to do, calls to make or things to pick up at the store. Now, I'm ready to make another kind of list. It's a list of things God has done for us, a blessings list.

Deuteronomy 4:9 says, *"Only be careful, and watch yourselves closely so that you do not forget the things your eyes have seen or let them fade from your heart as long as you live. Teach them to your children and to their children after them."* Do not forget! If we write down our blessings or certain Bible verses that help us, we're more likely to remember them. If we keep them in front of our eyes, they're more likely to get into our hearts. We should write clearly and in large letters so that, even if we just glance at the list, we'll see something that can change our outlook. We need to remember God, who he is and what he's done for us.

In Psalm 77, David was in a really bad way. He couldn't sleep. He said his soul would not be comforted. He asked such questions as:

- Has the Lord rejected me forever?
- Will he never show me favor?
- Is his unfailing love gone forever?
- Have his promises failed?
- Has God forgotten to be kind?

- Has he slammed the door on compassion?

Haven't we felt that way? I certainly can identify with David. After those questions, though, comes the word "Selah," which means "pause and consider." Think of that. Then, as if a light bulb has just gone off above his head, a change occurs, and David says:

"I will recall all you have done, O Lord. I remember your deeds of long ago. They are constantly in my thoughts. O God, your ways are holy. Is there any God as mighty as you? You are the God of miracles and wonders. You demonstrate your power among the nations. You have redeemed your people by your strength."
—Psalm 77:11-15 NLT

What a change in David's attitude, his emotions, and his outlook! We need our own Selah—a pause, an interlude to stop and consider who God is and what he's done for us. We need to write it down so we won't forget, or so that when we do forget, we can quickly see the list and remember once again.

Even when we do forget about God and his blessings, he doesn't forget about us. He's not waiting for us to think about him so that he can "fuss" at us or punish us. In Isaiah 49:15-16 (NLT), God says,

"Can a mother forget her nursing child? Can she feel no love for the child she has borne? But even if that were possible, I would not forget you! See, I have written your name on the palms of my hands."

That's amazing! Since God writes about us on his hand, let's write about him. Now look at this, the second half of Hebrews 13:5 from *The Amplified Bible.*

"He (God) himself has said, I will not in any way fail you nor give you up nor leave you without support. I will not, I will not, I will not in any degree leave you helpless nor forsake nor let you down or relax My hold on you. Assuredly not!"

That great scripture is worth reading several times this week.

And here's more "homework." Read Psalm 103, which begins, "*Bless the Lord, O my soul, and all that is within me bless His Holy Name. Bless the Lord, O, my soul, and forget not all His benefits (or all the good things he has done for us*" (Psalm 103:1-2 MEV). See how many good things David lists in the Psalm. Since God never changes, those same good things, those benefits, are not just for David, they're for us too.

Make a list of the ways God has blessed you. You'll be glad you did.

chapter sixty-four

Better Than a Hundred Grand

Money is a big subject in most people's lives. We have too little of it, so we have lots of worries. Or we have too much of it, so we have lots of worries. Proverbs provides perspective with this prayer.

> *"God, give me neither poverty nor riches! Give me just enough to sat-isfy my needs. For if I grow rich, I may deny you and say, 'Who is the Lord?' And if I am too poor, I may steal and insult God's holy name."*
> —Proverbs 30:8-9 NLT

The question is, "What is enough?" Is a hundred grand enough? How about a million? A billion? The truth with money, no matter how little or how much one has, is that enough is never enough.

When I was a child, a popular Sunday afternoon activity was to drive over to the "Country Club Section" of town and admire the big houses and the lush lawns and gardens. My parents pointed out the fancy features, but would almost always make some sad comment about the people who lived there. They had a wild kid who was always in trouble, they'd suffered a major illness, or they'd been through some sordid scandal. In other words, having money hadn't made them happy.

This conclusion somehow made us feel better, softening our envy perhaps. It made not having that kind of money easier to accept, because we were happier than those who had it. Eventually, this became a family joke. When we drove by huge homes, admired someone's fancy Ferrari, or saw pictures of glamorous, well-dressed, bejeweled celebrities, we'd say, "But you *know* they're not happy!" Of course, the truth was that those people could have been very happy, because happiness has little to do with how much or how little money we have.

What does God say about money?

"For the love of money is a root of all kinds of evil. Some people, eager for money, have wandered from the faith and pierced themselves with many griefs" (1 Timothy 6:10).

Give that some thought. So many evil things in our society exist primarily because they're financially profitable for someone: drugs, pornography, violent movies or video games, powerful insiders robbing the little guy and the shareholders. But the book of Proverbs warns, *"Do not wear yourself out to get rich; do not trust your own cleverness. Cast but a glance at riches, and they are gone, for they will surely sprout wings and fly off to the sky like an eagle"* (Proverbs 23:4-5).

Some of us have experienced that feeling. Our money took flight like a bird. We've learned first-hand that our worth, our security, our happiness, and our trust cannot be in money.

"Command those who are rich in this present world not to be arrogant nor to put their hope in wealth, which is so uncertain, but to put their hope in God, who richly provides us with everything for our enjoyment" (1 Timothy 6:17).

All these scriptures tell us that trusting God and seeking his wisdom are more important than desiring and striving for riches. I've listened to people who were out of work tell me that their situation brought them closer to God. They prayed more, drew closer to their families, and saw God working in their lives. Knowing God better, and serving him, is to be truly rich, regardless of our financial circumstances.

We want to trust God, seek His wisdom, and lay up treasures in heaven where they are truly secure. No one can take them from us. No one can steal our prayers, our praise to God, our love for our families and our friends, or our thanksgiving for what he has given us.

These things are worth far more than a hundred grand!

chapter sixty-five

Building Altars

I n the Old Testament, the Israelites built altars where they made sacrifices. Often these altars memorialized encounters with the Lord.

- In Geneses 12, when God rewarded Abram's obedience and
  gave him land, Abram built an altar.
- In Geneses 26, when God spoke to Isaac saying, *"Fear not, for
  I am with you,"* Isaac built an altar.
- In Genesis 35, God told Jacob to go to Bethel and make an
  altar, which Jacob did.
- In Exodus 17, after a great victory, Moses built an altar and
  named it, "The Lord Is My Banner." It was a reminder that
  God had given them victory.

You and I can follow the example of Abram, Isaac, and Moses by
building altars in our hearts and minds to remind us of the times God has
been with us, or helped us, or given us a victory. We need to remember
all the times he has demonstrated his love for us.

Sometimes, though, before those Israelites could build an altar, they
had to tear down altars that had been built to false gods. In Deuteronomy 7:5, God gave these instructions, *"This is what you are to do to them:
Break down their altars, smash their sacred stones, cut down their Asherah poles
and burn their idols in the fire."* Hmmm! These scriptures "set me to thinking." (That's what we do in the South.) During my lifetime I've built a
few altars to false gods. What about you? Have we worshipped money,
recognition, family, self? (I particularly struggle with the "I Want My

Way" Altar. If so, we have our work cut out for us, because God says, *"You shall have no other God before* (or beside) *me"* (Exodus 20:3).

Altars were also places where sacrifices were offered to God. Sacrifice isn't a very popular subject. Jesus said, *"If you are offering your gift at the altar and there remember that your brother or sister has something against you, leave your gift there in front of the altar. First go and be reconciled to them; then come and offer your gift"* (Matthew 5:23-24). Oh my! This is so important and so hard! We are supposed to make things right before we worship God. We need to seek forgiveness from those we have hurt or offended, and forgive those who have hurt or offended us. I think doing those two things helps clean out our pipeline of worship, making a clear way for our prayers to God. If our prayers seem to "stop at the ceiling," we probably have some forgiving to do and some apologies to make.

In the Old Testament, animals were killed and offered as sacrifices on the altar for forgiveness of sin. Let me remind you that Jesus is the final sacrifice for sin. That work is finished. God doesn't require the shedding of blood for us to gain forgiveness or receive anything else from him. When Jesus died on the cross, that sort of sacrifice was over. However, there are still sacrifices we can make. Hebrews 13:15-16 says, *"Through Jesus, therefore, let us continually offer to God a sacrifice of praise...And do not forget to do good and to share with others, for with such sacrifices God is pleased."*

And so, when it comes to altars, we have a "to do" list:

- Tear down those altars where we worship anyone or anything other than God.
- Build altars in our hearts and minds to remind us of the great things God has done.
- Forgive others and ask for forgiveness.
- Make our own sacrifices of prayer, praise, good deeds, and sharing.

If we do these things — you know what? We're going to be pleasing to God!

chapter sixty-six

Band-Aids and Biscuits

I love to cook! I grew up in a time when women cooked every day. Food was something we shared.

- If someone suffered a loss, we took food to the house (often fried chicken and pound cake).
- If someone was sick, we made soup and homemade biscuits.
- If someone had lots of out-of-town company coming, we cooked them a ham, a mess of green beans from the garden, and maybe some deviled eggs.

Doing this was easy for me, an inherited gift from God, a talent I enjoyed using. One day I began to belittle my gift in front of my daughter. She really got after me, saying, "Mom, don't you know that if God makes you good at something, you're supposed to do it over and over again until he tells you to do something else?" Cooking is my way of lending aid to a friend in need. Even though it looks insignificant to me at times, it's one of the ways God has equipped me to serve. And 1 Corinthians 12 has plenty to say about the different ways we are created to serve. You might want to read the entire chapter of 1 Corinthians 12 on your own. I'm going to share just part of it with you.

> *"Just as a body, though one, has many parts, but all its many parts form one body, so it is with Christ.... If the whole body were an eye, where would the sense of hearing be? If the whole body were an ear, where would the sense of smell be? But in fact God has placed the parts in the*

body, every one of them, just as he wanted them to be...The eye cannot say to the hand, "I don't need you!" And the head cannot say to the feet, "I don't need you!" ...If one part suffers, every part suffers with it; if one part is honored, every part rejoices with it. Now you are the body of Christ, and each of you is a part of it."

In other words:

- Clearly, we're not all alike. We don't all have the same job to do, the same gifts or talents, but all of us are necessary.
- We've each been made according to God's creative plan, and we're meant to work with what he's given us. It's our job to keep our particular part of the body strong, rather than letting it weaken from lack of use.
- No one person is more or less important than any other. The sooner we realize that, the sooner the body will function as it should.
- When one member of the group hurts, the whole group suffers with it. (If you've ever kicked your little toe, you know how such a seemingly unimportant part can affect the rest of your body.)

Here's the most important lesson of all. Each member of the body has the privilege of coming to the aid of the hurting member. If the little toe is in pain, the foot turns a little to take the pressure off the toe, and the leg takes on more of the work of walking (or hobbling). We need to take care of one another, to bear each other's burdens, and use whatever God has given us to help those in trouble, in pain, or in distress.

How do we do that? By using our gifts.

- If you're a gifted listener, listen. Pain often needs to be vented to an understanding ear.
- If you're good at a sport, use your talent to teach someone else.

- If you can throw a ball well, get a bunch of kids out to play. Recreation is important to good health.
- And all of us can pray.

We're sometimes tempted to think that just praying, just mentioning someone's name and need to God is, well, too simple. Does it really help? Here's a good way to think about that. When a part of the physical body is wounded or has an infection of some kind, extra white blood cells rush to the hurting or infected area. The cells fight the infection. When we pray, we are like those white blood cells going to the area that needs help. We're fighting against the bad stuff that doesn't belong in the spiritual body. The more white blood cells the better! The thought that we're in battle together encourages us to pray and to ask others to pray for those who have needs.

We all can do something with what we have to meet needs and to bless someone else. We need to BAND together to AID each other. A corny thought? Perhaps, but it reminds us of the importance of using our gifts, no matter how insignificant they may seem to us.

John Wesley, the founder of the Methodist church, is credited with saying, "Do all the good you can, by all the means you can, in all the ways you can, in all the places you can, at all the times you can, to all the people you can, as long as you ever can." Together, we can serve God by serving one another.

chapter sixty-seven

How to Be Happy

I have a few funny questions for you today.

- Why do people constantly return to the refrigerator with the hope that something new will have materialized?
- Is it true that the only difference between a yard sale and a trash pick-up is how close to the road the stuff is placed?
- Why don't we ever hear father-in-law jokes?
- If you take NyQuil and NoDoz at the same time, will you dream you couldn't sleep?

Life is full of questions, and today we're going to explore a common one. How can we be happy? A good start is to be ready to laugh at life and at ourselves. We need to look for the humorous side of things. Laughter doesn't solve our problems, but it can make them easier to bear for a while.

I used to hand out Laffy Taffy to my friends. I love that name. I could change it to Laffy Tuffy, because we need to laugh even when times are hard. We need deep, belly laughs in our lives. They're truly good for us. Proverbs 17:22 (AMP) says, "*A happy heart is good medicine and a cheerful mind works healing.*" Most of us think we can be happy only when things are going well, but the Bible tells us how to be happy Christians no matter what.

The Amplified Bible uses the word "happy" as a synonym for the word "blessed." Let me give you some of the words and phrases that go into the meaning of blessed in the Hebrew and the Greek. Blessed:

happy, spiritually prosperous, filled with joy or satisfied regardless of circumstances, happy because of the experience of God's favor and grace.

So, in looking to be happy, we can look at how to be blessed. The book of Psalms tell us that blessed or happy is the man (or woman) who:

- is forgiven of sin (32:1).
- trusts and takes refuge in the Lord (34:8).
- helps the poor and weak (41:1).
- continually sings praises to God (84:4).
- fears the Lord and delights in obeying him (112:1).

Proverbs says those are blessed who

- keep God's ways (8:32).
- listen to God (8:34).

And Matthew chapter five lists these qualities of a happy person:

- aware of a need for God
- gentle and lowly
- desiring righteousness
- merciful
- pure in heart
- peacemaking
- persecuted for following God

Obviously, God has plenty of advice for us on how to be happy. I want to stress just two ways today. First, we need to be happy and thankful for a heavenly Father who loves us enough to discipline and correct us. Sometimes, when things are hard for me, when I am not getting my own way about things, I can almost hear God saying, "I'm allowing this situation only for your own good, because I love you. You need to change something in your life. I want you to be happy, and you will never be happy or have joy on the path you are following right now. Come on, follow me."

Psalm 94:12 (AMP) says, "*Blessed (happy, fortunate, to be envied) is the man whom God disciplines and instructs.*" How could that be true? The answer is in Hebrews 12:11, this time quoted from the New Living Translation, "*No discipline is enjoyable while it is happening--it's painful! But afterward there will be a peaceful harvest of right living for those who are trained in this way.*" So, as odd as it may sound, we need to be happy that God will discipline us.

Here's a second way the Bible tells us we can be happy and blessed. "*Blessed are all who fear the Lord, who walk in obedience to him. You will eat the fruit of your labor; blessings and prosperity will be yours*" (Psalm 128:1-2).

What does this tell us we should do? Fear and follow. To fear God is to acknowledge who he is, the Almighty God, and to worship him. To follow God is to be obedient to his Word and to emulate Jesus. Will that be hard? Yes, because our flesh is weak and rebellious, and because Satan does not want us to be happy. But Jesus wants us to be happy, to be blessed and full of joy. In John 15, after teaching his disciples many things, Jesus told them (and those of us who desire to follow him) the purpose of his commandments. Verse 11 (AMP) says, "*I have told you these things, that My joy and delight may be in you, and that your joy and gladness may be of full measure and complete and overflowing.*"

How can we become happy Christians? A full answer to that question would surely fill at least one book. These principles don't cover everything, but they're a great place to start:

- Worship God.
- Obey his commands.
- Receive his discipline.
- Follow his instructions.

And do it all with joy.

Handouts for Each Devotional

The devotionals you've just read were a joint effort for my parents. Every week, Mom would write, practice, and deliver her talk with great humor and enthusiasm. Dad was in charge of typing up her speaking notes and preparing the handout for each lesson.

Oh, those handouts! These were not your ordinary sheets of paper filled with notes and questions. Dad would print out hundreds of tag board cards, carefully cut to pocket size. Each one reinforced Mom's key points and cited related Bible verses. Then, together, my parents would attach some little item that was associated with the devotional—a coin, a rock, maybe a piece of candy or a small length of yarn—to each card. If all else failed, they could almost always find a sticker that related to the lesson. Most of the items came from a grocery store or craft store. Others they ordered on-line at Oriental Trading Company. Many times, they slipped the items into small 2x3 inch zipper locking plastic bags, then stapled the bags to the printed cards.

These creative takeaways added a whole new dimension to the phrase "object lesson." I've been told that people carry those cards around in pockets and purses long after they've heard Mom speak at Between Jobs Ministries. What follows is a description of those handouts. Permission is granted for you to reproduce them for your own devotional presentations. (As you will see, Mom loves chocolate. This was her chance to distribute plenty of it!) May you enjoy the great privilege of handing out the Word of God.

1. Pure Gold

- "The law from your mouth is more precious to me than thousands of pieces of silver and gold" (Psalm 119:72 NIV). (David praying to God)
- "Blessed are those who find wisdom, those who gain understanding, for she is more profitable than silver and yields better returns than gold" (Proverbs 3:13-14 NIV).

Homework: Study 2 Timothy 3:16-17.

(Handout Item: Gold-wrapped chocolate)

2. A Stake in the Ground

We are made new: "To all who believe in Him and accept Him, He gave the right to become children of God. They are reborn! This is not a physical birth resulting from human passion or plan – this rebirth comes from God" (John 1:12-13 NLT).

We are renewed: "Be constantly renewed in the spirit of your mind, having a fresh mental and spiritual attitude, and put on the new nature created in God's image in true righteousness and holiness" (Ephesians 4:23-24 AMP).

(Handout Item: A toothpick or small Popsicle stick)

3. A Different Diet

Chocolate is yummy. Sugar is sweet. But it's the Word of God, we need to eat.

(Handout Item: Any kind of chocolate)

4. Happy Hearts

Laffy Taffy (or Snickers) might help, but a happy heart needs to be:

- Full of forgiveness (Psalm 32:1)
- Full of thankfulness (Psalm 100:4)
- Full of trust (Psalm 32:10)
- Quick to obey (James 1:22)

"He who has a glad heart has a continual feast (regardless of circumstances)" (Proverbs 15:15 AMP).

(Handout Item: Laffy Taffy or Snickers)

5. Mustard Seeds

- "Jesus said: 'If you had faith as small as a mustard seed, you could say to this mountain, 'move from here to there' and it would move. Nothing would be impossible'" (Matthew 17:20 NLT).
- "For it is by grace you have been saved, through faith" (Ephesians 2:8 NIV).

Grow the seed! Read Hebrews 11:1, Romans 10:17, Ephesians 3:16-17.

(Handout Item: A mustard seed, purchased from
the spice section of a grocery store)

6. The Very Best Valentine

The first Valentine message is still the best one ever sent!
For God so loved… John 3:16

(Handout Item: any Valentine item)

7. Love Muscles

Give more Hugs & Kisses. Go and show more love.
Read 1 Corinthians 13:4-6.

(Handout Item: Hershey's Hugs and Kisses)

8. What Color Is Your Tongue?

Change the color of your tongue, not with *candy* – but with
God's Word.

Jesus prayed, "Sanctify them by the truth; your word is
truth" (John 17:17 NIV).

Speak the truth.
Speak the word.
Change the tongue.
Change the life.

(Handout Item: Jawbreaker candy)

9. Out of Control

You can Snicker when life is a Cruncher, knowing:

E G B O K B G I I C.

"'For I know the plans I have for you,' says the Lord. 'They are plans for good and not for disaster, to give you a future and a hope'" (Jeremiah 29:11 NLT).

Homework: Give God control. He knows the way.

(Handout item: Nestlé's Crunch or Snicker's Bar)

10. Double-minded

Let's not be double-minded!

"If any of you lacks wisdom, you should ask God, who gives generously to all without finding fault, and it will be given to you. But when you ask, you must believe and not doubt, because the one who doubts is like a wave of the sea, blown and tossed by the wind. That person should not expect to receive anything from the Lord. Such a person is double-minded and unstable in all they do."

—James 1:5-8 NIV

Homework: Practice Philippians 4:8,

"And now, dear brothers and sisters, one final thing. Fix your thoughts on what is true, and honorable, and right, and pure, and lovely, and admirable. Think about things that are excellent and worthy of praise."

(Handout item: Dubble Bubble gum)

11. A Joyful Noise

- "Open my lips, Lord, and my mouth will declare your praise" (Psalm 51:15 NIV).
- "Because your loving kindness is better than life, my lips shall praise you. So will I bless you while I live; I will lift up my hands in your name. My whole being shall be satisfied as with marrow and fatness; and my mouth shall praise you with joyful lips" (Psalm 63:3-5 AMP).
- "Through Him, therefore, let us at all times offer up to God a sacrifice of praise, which is the fruit of lips that thankfully acknowledge and confess and glorify His name" (Hebrews 13:15 AMP).

Homework: Read and enjoy 2 Chronicles, chapter 20.

(Handout item: Wax lips or lip-shaped whistle)

12. No More Excuses

"I can do everything with the help of Christ who gives me the strength I need" (Philippians 4:13).

Do the last thing you can remember thinking God wanted you to do, that you did not do.

(Handout item: Dum Dum lollipop)

13. No More Foolishness

- "The fear of the Lord is the beginning of knowledge, but fools despise wisdom and discipline" (Proverbs 1:7 NIV).
- "Through skillful and Godly wisdom is a house (a life, a home, a family) built, and by understanding it is established on a sound and good foundation" (Proverbs 24:3 AMP).

(Handout item: Smarties candy)

14. F.R.O.G.

Fully Rely On God
- "If anyone acknowledges that Jesus is the Son of God, God lives in them and they in God. And so we know and RELY on the love God has for us" (1 John 4:15-16 NIV).
- "Lord Almighty, blessed is the one who trusts in you" (Psalms 84:12 NIV).
- "God is our Refuge and our Strength, an ever present help in trouble" (Psalm 46:1 NIV).

Homework: Read and enjoy the "By Faith" chapter, Hebrews 11.

(Handout item: Plastic frog from Oriental
Trading Company, or a frog sticker)

15. No Fear

Don't be haunted by fear. Fear not!

- "For God has not given us a spirit of fear (timidity or cowardice, of craven and clinging fear), but He has given us a spirit of power and of love and of a calm and well balanced mind and discipline and self-control" (2 Timothy 1:7 AMP).
- "You did not receive a spirit that makes you a slave again to fear, but you received the spirit of sonship whereby we cry 'Abba Father'" (Romans 8:15 NIV).

(Handout item: Halloween sticker or candy)

16. Under His Wings

- "How priceless is your unfailing love, O God! People take refuge in the shadow of your wings" (Psalm 36:7 NIV).
- "He will cover you with His feathers, and under his wings you will find refuge; his faithfulness will be your shield and rampart" (Psalm 91:4 NIV).

Homework: Psalm 61:4 (Read and enjoy the whole Psalm.)

(Handout item: Feather)

17. Filtered Through Faith

Filter your life through faith

"And without faith it is impossible to please God, because anyone who comes to him must believe that he exists and that he rewards those who earnestly seek him" (Hebrews 11:6 NIV).

(Handout item: Coffee filter)

18. Yellow Ribbons

Forgiveness is:

- A great gift to *receive*: "All the prophets testify about him (Christ) that everyone who believes in him receives forgiveness of sins through his name" (Acts 10:43 NIV).
- A great gift to *give*: "Bear with each other and forgive one another if any of you has a grievance against someone. Forgive as the Lord forgave you" (Colossians 3:13 NIV).
- A great prayer to *ask*: "May I be kind, tenderhearted and forgiving even as God for Christ's sake has forgiven me" (Ephesians 4:32, author's paraphrase).

(Handout item: Yellow ribbon)

19. Eye Level

- In his perfect love, God wills what is best for us. (Proverbs 3:5-6)
- In his perfect wisdom, he knows what is best for us. (1 Corinthians 1:25)
- In his perfect sovereignty, he has the power to bring it about. (Matthew 28:18)

God gives his best to those who leave the choice to him, so let God choose!

(Handout item: Chewing gum or a chewy candy)

20. The Fretnotters' Club

- Matthew 6:25 – Don't worry about everyday life.
- Matthew 6:27 – Worry doesn't change anything.
- Matthew 6:34 – Take one day at a time.
- I Peter 5:7 – Give all your worries and cares to God, because he cares about what happens to you.
- Philippians 4:6 – Do not fret or worry about anything; instead, pray about everything, and thank him for all he has done.

(Handout item: The words above printed on stiff paper
cut to represent a membership card.)

21. Never Forgotten

"I love you this much."

(Handout item: Cross sticker, or print the words above
on a card cut out in the shape of a cross.)

22. Amazingly Able

God is amazingly able

- To keep his word and to do what he promises. (Romans 4:21)
- To generously provide all we need so we will be able to share with others. (2 Corinthians 9:8)
- To guard what we entrust to him. (2 Timothy 1:12)
- To save completely those who come to him. (Hebrews 7:25)
- To keep us from falling. (Jude 24)

"God is able (to carry out His purpose and) to do super abundantly, far over and above all that we dare to ask or think" Ephesians 3:20 (AMP).

(Handout item: Small toy maze)

23. Our Gardener

- Best place for roots: In his love (Ephesians 3:17)
- Best water source: His Word (Ephesians 5:26)
- Miracle-growing plant food: His faithfulness (Psalm 37:3)
- Feeding schedule: At the proper time (Psalm 145:15)
- Pruning tool: His teachings (John 15:1-3)
- Best covering mulch: Love (1 Peter 4:8)
- Best plant protection: His Power (1 Peter 1:5)

Remember, all plants need Sonshine. Get into his presence. (Numbers 6:24-26)

Homework: Read Psalm 121.

(Handout item: Sunflower seed)

24. Lifesavers

God's grace is our life saver!

- He saves us eternally. "For it is by grace you have been saved" (Ephesians 2:8 NIV).
- He saves us daily. "For the grace of God has appeared that offers salvation to all people. It teaches us to say "No" to ungodliness and worldly passions, and to live self-controlled, upright and godly lives in this present age" (Titus 2:11-12 NIV).

(Handout item: Individually wrapped Lifesavers candy)

25. Precious Pearls

You are a pearl of great value, purchased by Jesus Christ.

- Matthew 13:45
- John 3:16

(Handout item: Fake pearl from craft store)

26. Sweeter than Honey

God's words are sweeter than honey.

- "How sweet are your words to my taste, sweeter than honey to my mouth" (Psalm 119:103 NIV).
- "My child, eat honey for it is good, and the honeycomb is sweet to the taste. In the same way, wisdom is sweet to your soul. If you find it, you will have a bright future, and your hopes will not be cut short" (Proverbs 24:13-14 NLT).

Homework: Read Psalm 19:7-10.

(Handout item: Bit-O-Honey candy)

27. Whose World Is It Anyway?

"To the Lord your God belong the heavens, even the highest heavens, the earth and everything in it" (Deuteronomy 10:14 NIV). Yet, out of all that, God chose you as the object of his love.

Homework: Read the proof, John 3:16-17.

(Handout item: Globe sticker or key chain of a globe)

28. No Bones about It

- Don't hold on to sin. Confess it, and receive forgiveness. "I shall be joyful in the Lord. I shall rejoice in His deliverance. All my bones shall say, 'Lord, who is like you?'" (Psalm 35:9-10 ESV).
- Trust in the Lord. "This will bring health to your body and nourishment to your bones" (Proverbs 3:8 NIV).
- Have a happy heart and a cheerful mind. "A crushed spirit dries up the bones" (Proverbs 17:22 NIV).

(Handout item: Bone Candy [available at Halloween] or Milk-Bone dog biscuit)

29. Heaven on Earth

"In the beginning God created the heavens and the earth" (Genesis 1:1 NIV).

Homework: Check out these verses about heaven:

- Psalm 19:1-4 tells of God's glory.
- Romans 1:20 fosters belief in God.
- 2 Corinthians 5:1 describes our eternal home.

(Handout item: Star stickers)

30. Freebies

Our salvation is a free gift, not a payday.

- "For the wages of sin is death, but the gift of God is eternal life through Jesus Christ our Lord" (Romans 6:23 NIV).
- "God saved you by his grace when you believed. And you can't take credit for this, it is a gift from God" (Ephesians 2:8 NLT).
- "Give and you will receive. Your gift will return to you in full—pressed down, shaken together to make room for more, running over, and poured back into your lap" (Luke 6:38 NLT).

(Handout item: PayDay candy bar,
but play money would also work.)

31. Faith Comes by Hearing

"Faith comes by hearing, and hearing by the word of Christ" (Romans 10:17 NASB).

How to hear God's Word, according to Proverbs 4:20-23:

- Pay attention.
- Listen.
- Focus your eyes.
- Let it into your heart.
- Guard your heart.

Matthew 12:34
- Speak his Word.

(Handout item: Bible sticker or scripture memory card)

32. Kicked Forward

I'm going forward.

- "I have strength for all things in Christ who empowers me. (I am ready for anything and equal to anything through Him who infuses inner strength into me. I am self-sufficient in Christ's sufficiency)" (Philippians 4:13 AMP).
- Paul says we can be "more than conquerors and gain a surpassing victory through Him (Christ) Who loved us" (Romans 8:37 AMP).

(Handout item: Kit Kat bar, because it sounds like "Kick At")

33. A Level Praying Field

- Same love - John 3:16, Romans 5:8
- Same forgiveness - 2 Peter 3:9, Acts 10:43
- Equally desired by God - Luke 15:8-10

We are his lost coins. He is searching for us.

(Handout Item: Coin)

34. Marvelous Mercy

"But God is so rich in mercy, and he loved us so much, that even though we were dead because of our sins, he gave us life when he raised Christ from the dead. (It is only by God's grace that you have been saved!)" (Ephesians 2:4-5 NLT).

Since we have received mercy, let's show mercy.

- Forgive someone even if he/she doesn't deserve it. (Neither do we.)
- Show compassion when someone makes a mistake. (We make mistakes all the time.)
- Be tender and sympathetic to the hurts of others.

"Be merciful (sympathetic, tender, responsive, and compassionate) just as your Father is merciful" (Luke 6:36 AMP).

(Handout item: Packet of M&M'S, standing for Marvelous Mercy)

35. September 11, 2002

"I urge you, first of all, to pray for all people. Ask God to help them; intercede on their behalf, and give thanks for them. Pray this way for kings and all who are in authority so that we can live peaceful and quiet lives marked by godliness and dignity" (1 Timothy 2: 1-2 NLT).

- Jesus said, "I am the light of the world" (John 8:12 NIV).
- Jesus said, "You are the light of the world" (Mathew 5:14 NIV).
- Jesus said, "Let your light so shine before men that they may see your good deeds and praise your Father in heaven" (Matthew 5:16 NIV).

(Handout item: Small birthday cake candle)

36. Magnification

Where is our focus?

- "I will bless the Lord at all times. His praise will continually be in my mouth. My life makes its boast in the Lord. Let the humble and afflicted hear and be glad. Oh, magnify the Lord with me, and let us exalt His name together" (Psalm 34:1-3 AMP).
- "Let all who seek You rejoice and be glad in You. And let those who love your salvation say continually, 'Let God be magnified!'" (Psalm 70:4 NASB).

(Handout item: Toy magnifying glass)

37. The Barnabas Bunch

(This handout is a "Barnabas Bunch Card" printed out on heavy paper with the words below.)

This Barnabas Bunch membership card entitles you to give and receive encouragement with love and compassion.
Additional power and advantages available to Bible readers. (Acts 20:32)

_____   _____

(Member Signature)   (Membership Date)

- Not valid until signed.
- Not valid if used in combination with pride or selfishness.
- No expiration date

38. Mounds of Treasure

Mound means to heap or pile up, so "Gather and heap up and store for yourselves treasures in heaven" (Matthew 6:20 AMP). Here are a few of our heavenly treasures:

- Proverbs 2:1-5 Wisdom and understanding
- Colossians 2:2-3 Wisdom and knowledge
- Proverbs 15:6 Righteousness
- Isaiah 33:6 Reverence and worship
- Matthew 13:52 Knowledge of God's Word
- Hebrews 11:25-26 What we suffer for Christ
- I Peter 1:3-7 Salvation

(Handout item: Mounds bar)

39. Coloring Book Prayers

"I will trust in the Lord with all my heart and I will not depend on my own understanding. I will seek his will in all I do, and he will direct my paths" (Proverbs 3:6-7 author's paraphrase).

Homework: Read Psalm 143. It's a wonderful prayer!

(Handout item: Crayon)

40. Always

What shall we do now, later and always?

- "Jesus told them a parable to the effect that they ought always to *pray* and not to turn coward (faint, lose heart, or give up)" (Luke 18:1 AMP).
- "Rejoice in the Lord *always*. I'll say it again: *Rejoice*" (Philippians 4:4 NIV).
- "See that no one pays back evil for evil, but always try to *do good* to each other and to all people. Always *be joyful*. Never stop praying. Be thankful in all circumstances, for this is God's will for you who belong to Christ Jesus" (1 Thessalonians 5:15-18 NLT).

Homework: Read Luke 18: 1-8, Romans 12: 12-21,
and Ephesians 4:31-32.

(Handout item: Now & Later candy chews)

41. Hold Fast

Hold fast to:

- What is good. (1 Thessalonians 5:21)
- Faith and a clean conscience. (1 Timothy 1:19)
- Wholesome and sound teaching. (2 Timothy 1:13-14)
- Your confession of faith in Christ Jesus. (Hebrews 4:14)

"Let us hold tightly without wavering to the hope we affirm, for God can be trusted to keep his promise. Let us think of ways to motivate one another to acts of love and good works" (Hebrews 10:23-24 NLT).

Homework: Be encouraged! Read Isaiah 41, verses 10 and 13.

(Handout item: Paper clip or small alligator clip)

42. Juicy Fruit

We were designed by God to produce fruit.

- In Romans 7:4 we learn that, if we have accepted Christ as our Savior, we have died to the law through the crucifixion of Christ. And now we belong to Him who was raised from the dead. As a result, we can bear fruit for God.
- Romans 8:9 (NLT) says, "You are not controlled by your sinful nature. You are controlled by the (Holy) Spirit if you have the Spirit of God living in you."
- These are the fruits the Holy Spirit produces in those born of the Spirit, according to Galatians 5:22: love, joy, peace, patience (an even temper), kindness, goodness, faithfulness, gentleness (kindness, humility), and self-control."

(Handout item: Juicy Fruit gum)

43. Punching Holes in the Darkness

- Jesus said, "I am the light of the world" (John 8:12 NIV).
- We are to be reflections of this light. "You are the light of the world – like a city on a mountain, glowing in the night for all to see. Don't hide your light under a basket! Instead, put it on a stand and let it shine for all. In the same way, let your good deeds shine out for all to see, so that everyone will praise your heavenly Father" (Mathew 5:14-16 NLT).

(Handout item: Single twinkle light bulb
from a strand of Christmas lights)

44. Refreshment

Webster's definition of refreshment: Drink, food, rest, new supplies, and a stimulated memory or a renewed mind.

- In John 7:37 (NIV), Jesus said, "Let anyone who is thirsty come to me and drink."
- In John 6:48 (NIV), Jesus said, "I am the bread of life."
- In Matthew 11:28 (AMP), Jesus said, "Come to me all you who labor and are heavy laden and overburdened, and I will cause you to rest. (I will ease and relieve and refresh your souls.)
- Philippians 4:19 (AMP) promises that, "God will liberally supply (fill to the full) your every need according to His riches in glory in Christ Jesus."
- Acts 3:19 (AMP) tells us to "Repent (change your mind and turn around and return to God), that your sins may be wiped out and times of refreshing may come from the Lord."

(Handout item: Mint)

45. All Grown Up

Be rooted in God's love.

"When I think of the wisdom and scope of God's plan, I fall to my knees and pray to the Father, the creator of everything in heaven and on earth. I pray that from his glorious, unlimited resources, he will give you mighty inner strength through his Holy Spirit. And I pray that Christ will be more at home in your hearts as you trust in him. May your roots go down deep into the soil of God's marvelous love, and may you have the power to understand, as all God's people should, how long, how high, and how deep his love really is. May you experience the love of Christ, though you will never fully understand it. Then you will be filled with fullness of life and power that comes from God."
—Ephesians 3:14-19 NLT

(Handout item: Sticker of a carrot)

46. Deep Roots

"And now, just as you accepted Christ Jesus as your Lord, you must continue to follow him. Let your roots grow down into him, and let your lives be built on him. Then your faith will grow strong in the truth you were taught, and you will overflow with thankfulness."
—Colossians 2:6-7 (NLT).

- Rooted in Christ.
- Rooted in God's Love.
- What a SWEET, JOYful place to be!

Homework: Read Psalm 1:3 and John 15:5.

(Handout item: Almond Joy)

47. Rope of Hope

The Lord says in Jeremiah 29:11 (NLT), "For I know the plans I have for you. They are plans for good and not for disaster, to give you a future and a hope."

Here are the strands of our rope of hope:
- God Himself: Psalm 39:7
- God's Word: Psalm 42:5
- Prayer: 1 Thessalonians 5:17-18
- Christian Friends: 1 Thessalonians 5:11
- The Holy Spirit: John 14:16

(Handout item: Small piece of thin rope from a hardware store)

48. You Reap What You Sow

Good Seed - Good Harvest

"Don't be misled. Remember that you can't ignore God and get away with it. You will always reap what you sow. Those who live to satisfy their own sinful desires will harvest the consequences of decay and death. But those who live to please the Spirit will harvest everlasting life. So, don't get tired of doing what is good. Don't get discouraged and give up, for we will reap a harvest of blessings at the appropriate time. Whenever we have the opportunity, we should do good to everyone, especially to our Christian brothers and sisters."
—Galatians 6:7-10 NLT

Homework: Forgive someone.

(Handout item: Sunflower seed)

49. American Idols

Are we doing the molding? 1 John 5:21 (AMP) warns us, "Little children, keep yourselves from idols (false gods), from anything and everything that would occupy the place in your heart due to God, from any substitute for Him that would take first place in your life."

Are we being molded? Isaiah 64:8 (NIV) teaches us to pray, "You, Lord, are our Father. We are the clay, you are the potter: we are all the works of your hand."

Homework: Read Exodus 20:3-4, Jeremiah 29:11, Jonah 2:8, and 2 Corinthians 4:6-7.

(Handout item: Play-Doh)

50. The Rock

"I waited patiently for the Lord; He turned to me and heard my cry. He lifted me out of the slimy pit, out of the mud and mire; He set my feet on a rock and gave me a firm place to stand."

—Psalm 40:1-2 NIV

"The Lord is my rock, my fortress and my deliverer; My God is my rock in whom I take refuge."

—Psalm 18:2 NIV

Homework: Check out these verses about our Rock:

- 1 Corinthians 10:4 The Rock – Christ
- Psalm 19:14 The Rock – Redeemer
- Ephesians 2:20 The Rock – The Cornerstone – Jesus

(Handout item: A pebble or rock)

51. Candy Canes

- Upside down, it is a shepherd's crook. (John 10:14)
- The J is for the name Jesus. (Philippians 2:9-11)
- The hardness of the candy reminds us that Jesus is the Rock. (Psalm 18:2)
- The white color stands for the purity of Jesus. (Hebrews 4:15)
- The peppermint flavor is a reminder of hyssop used for cleansing. (Psalm 51:7)
- The red stripes represent the blood of Jesus. (Romans 3:21-25)

Let us be Joyful in Jesus because of who he is and what he has done for us.

(Handout item: Candy cane)

52. The Gift Exchange

- We give our belief and receive eternal life.
- We give our sins and receive forgiveness.
- We give our inconsistencies and receive God's permanent grace.
- We give our weakness and weariness and receive God's strength and power.

God's best gift is our Savior, Jesus Christ.

(Handout item: Christmas gift tag)

53. The Stirring Spoon

- Let's continue to look into the mirrors of our souls to examine our reactions to life's stirring spoons.
- Let's give our reactions to Christ. He will mold us into his image (Romans 8:29) so that we can shine like jewels for him.
- Smile. You have God's seal of approval. (2 Corinthians 1:21-22)

(Handout item: Plastic spoon)

54. Continue Stirring

What do we do when God uses his stirring spoons?

- Thank God for the opportunity to get rid of self.
- Thank God for the person (or situation) used to bring out our reactions and ask God to bless them.
- Give our reactions to Jesus. Name them and forget it. (He died for it.)
- Repent and be truly sorry (because we really want to be like Jesus wants us to be.)
- Ask Jesus to fill this empty space with himself and with the fruit of the Holy Spirit.
- Thank him again and let him change us.

Homework: Study these scriptures: 1 Thessalonians 5:18, Romans 8:28-29, and Colossians 3:5.

(Handout item: Plastic spoon)

55. Like a Yo-yo

The yo-yo life doesn't work. This works:

- Trust in our steadfast (non-yo-yoing) God. "Lean on, trust in, and be confident in the Lord with all your heart and mind and do not rely on your own insight or understanding" (Proverbs 3:5 AMP).
- Be steadfast in prayer. "Be earnest and unwearied and steadfast in your prayer life, being both alert and intent in your praying with thanksgiving" (Colossians 4:2 AMP).
- Be steadfast in doing God's will. "Therefore my beloved brethren, be firm, steadfast, immovable, always abounding in the work of the Lord (always being superior, excelling, doing more than enough in the service of the Lord), knowing and being continually aware that your labor in the Lord is not futile (it is never wasted or to no purpose)" (1 Corinthians 15:58 AMP).

Homework: Read Psalms 111-112,
1 John 1:9 and Romans 11:29.

(Handout item: Yo-yo)

56. A Tangled Mess

Are the threads of our lives tangled up? Do we feel trapped or imprisoned?

Jesus declared in Luke 4:21 that he fulfilled this scripture from Isaiah 61:1 (NIV), "The Spirit of the Sovereign Lord is on me because the Lord has appointed me to bring good news to the poor. He has sent me to comfort the broken hearted, to proclaim freedom for the captives and release from darkness for the prisoners."

Homework: Read John 8:31-32, Hebrews 12:1,
John 8:36 and Romans 8.

(Handout item: Wad of thread)

57. Tongue Suppressors

"Set a guard over my mouth, Lord; keep watch over the door of my lips" (Psalm 141:3 NIV).

"The tongue has the power of life and death, and those who love it will eat its fruit" (Proverbs 18:21 NIV).

(Handout item: Large craft stick. We printed these
verses and glued them on each stick.)

58. Trust

It's what's inside that counts. May we have trust deep down inside!

"The Lord is my Strength and my Shield; My heart TRUSTS in (relies on and confidently leans on) Him, and I am helped; therefore, my heart greatly rejoices, and with my song will I praise Him."
—Psalm 28:7 AMP

Homework: Read Psalms 62 and 112.

(Handout item: Tootsie Pop)

59. Two Cents Worth

We are to give because we love God and others, not for show or reward.

Nothing we give is too small for God to use in his kingdom. God makes our little into much.

Homework: Read about the widow's mite in Mark 12:41-44.

(Handout item: Two pennies)

60. What Are You Looking At?

Looking back? Psalm 77:11-12 (NIV) proclaims, "I will remember the deeds of the Lord; yes, I will remember your miracles of long ago. I will consider all of your works and meditate on your mighty deeds."

Looking around? 2 Corinthians 4:18 (NIV) instructs us to "fix our eyes not on what is seen, but what is unseen, since what is seen is temporary, but what is unseen is eternal."

Looking ahead? Psalm 141:8 (NIV) teaches us to pray, "My eyes are fixed on you, Sovereign Lord; in you I take refuge."

Behold! "Behold (regard and keep what is about to be said in your gaze, pay attention now) I stand at the door and knock; if anyone hears my voice and opens the door, I will come in to him and dine with him and he with Me" (Revelation 3:20 AMP).

(Handout item: Googly eyes)

61. Whatcha Got?

Five loaves and two fish —
So little to us.
So much in God's hands.
What do you have?
Go and see!
(Then read Mark 6:30-44.)

(Handout item: Swedish fish or loaves and fishes candy packets)

62. Nip It in the Bud

What shall we do with sin? Nip it in the bud. How?

Recognize that we are sinners. "For all have sinned and fall short of the glory of God" (Romans 3:23 NIV).

Repent of the sin. "Repent, then, and turn to God, so that your sins may be wiped out, that a time of refreshing may come from the Lord" (Acts 3:19 NIV).

Receive God's forgiveness. "Then I acknowledged my sin to you and did not cover up my iniquity. I said, 'I will confess my transgressions to the Lord.' And you forgave the guilt of my sin" (Psalm 32:5 NIV).

Reckon ourselves dead to the sin. Count (reckon) yourselves dead to sin but alive to God in Christ Jesus" (Romans 6:11 NIV).

Rejoice because we are not slaves to sin. (We win.) "For every child of God defeats this evil world" by trusting Christ to give the victory (1John 5:4 NLT).

Homework: Read Romans 6:12-14.

(Handout item: Nips candy)

63. Write It Down

Remember God: "I will remember the deeds of the Lord. Yes! I will remember your miracles of long ago. I will consider all your works and meditate on all your mighty deeds" (Psalm 77:11-12 NIV).

God remembers you: "He, God Himself, has said, I will not in any way fail you nor give you up nor leave you without support. I will not, I will not, I will not, in any degree leave you helpless nor forsake, let you down, or relax my hold on you. Assuredly not!" (Hebrews 13:5b AMP).

Homework: Study Psalm 103 and write down
the benefits David lists. They are for us too!

(Handout item: Golf pencil)

64. Better Than a Hundred Grand

- "Happy is the person who finds wisdom and gains under-standing. For the profit of wisdom is better than silver, and her wages are better than gold" (Proverbs 3:13-14 NLT).
- "Search for wisdom and understanding as you would for lost money or hidden treasure" (Proverbs 2:4 NLT).
- "Don't store up treasures here on earth, where they can be eaten by moths and get rusty, and where thieves break in and steal. Store up your treasures in heaven, where they will never become moth eaten or rusty and where they will be safe from thieves. Wherever your treasure is, there will your heart and thoughts also be" (Wisdom from Jesus, Matthew 6:19-21 NLT).

Homework: Ask yourself these questions: What am I storing up in heaven? Am I a rich person in heaven?

(Handout item: Play money or 100 Grand chocolate bar)

65. Building Altars

A stone for your altar to the King of Kings:

My altar of remembrance:
  God helped me to _____
  God was with me when _____
My altar to be destroyed:
  To the false God of _____
A person I need to forgive_____
A person from whom I need to seek forgiveness _____
Sacrifices and gifts I can offer to God_____

"With Jesus' help, let us continually offer our sacrifices of praise to God by proclaiming the glory of his name. Don't forget to do good and to share what you have with those in need, for such sacrifices are pleasing to God" (Hebrews 13:15-16 NLT).

(Handout item: rock)

66. Band-Aids and Biscuits

Let's Band together to Aid the hurting.

"Share each other's burdens, and in this way obey the law of Christ. So let's not get tired of doing what is good. At just the right time we will reap a harvest of blessing if we don't give up. Therefore, whenever we have the opportunity, we should do good to everyone, especially to those in the family of faith."
—Galatians 6:2, 9-10 NLT

(Handout Item: Band-Aid)

67. How to Be Happy

Be Happy! Don't just *SNICKER*. Rejoice and laugh out loud.

"Be happy in your faith and rejoice and be glad-hearted continually. Be unceasing in prayer. Thank God in everything no matter what the circumstances may be, for this is the will of God for you who are in Christ Jesus"

—1Thessalonians 5:16-18 AMP

Homework: Be happy and thankful for God's discipline and correction. (Psalm 94:12.)

Be happy as you fear God and follow his ways. (Read Psalm 128:1-2.)

(Handout item: Smiley face sticker)

Endnotes

1 Words by Judson W. Vand de Venter, "I Surrender All," 1896.

2 (http://www.quotesvalley.com/Were-all-here-for-a-spell-get-all-the-good-laughs-you-can-3/) accessed 7/14/2015.

3 (http://www.catholicsentinel.org/main.asp?SectionID=2&Sub-SectionID=35&ArticleID=4175, 1999) accessed 7/14/2015.

4 John H. Sammis, "Trust and Obey," 1887.

5 Taken from: *The World's Greatest Collection of Clean Jokes*, copyright © 1998 by Bob Phillips, Published by Harvest House Publishers, Eugene, Oregon 97402, www.harvesthousepublishers.com. Used by permission.

6 Paraphrased from an old story published in the June 14, 1895 issue of the New York Times. (http://www.query.nytimes.com) accessed 9/30/15.

7 This story has been reprinted in various forms over the years, including the *New York Post* on October 14, 1971.

8 Barbara Johnson, *Splashes of Joy* (New York: Thomas Nelson, 2000), 332.

9 Robert Robinson, "Come, Thou Fount of Every Blessing," 1758.

10 Bill Hybels, *Too Busy Not to Pray* (Downers Grove, IL: InterVarsity Press, 2008), 26.

11 Found on a variety of websites as an uncredited joke. For example: (http://www.christian-jokes.net/Jokes/Heaven-and-Hell-Jokes/216-100-points-to-get-into-Heaven.aspx) accessed 6/6/15.

12 John Newton, "Amazing Grace," 1779.

13 Derek Prince, *Extravagant Love* (Ft. Lauderdale: Derek Prince Ministries, 1985).

14 Source not found.

15 E. Stanley Jones, *The Way to Power and Praise* (Nashville, TN: Abingdon Press, 1949, 1978) 203.

16 (http://www.snopes.com/glurge/brownies.asp), accessed 6/2/2015, reported that, "Our earliest sighting of this item comes from an August 2001 web site posting, and it has since appeared in at least one book. However, even in its earliest incarnation the author was not identified, which makes it difficult to determine whether the story is a true account or a work of fiction." This author found it uncredited on several websites.

17 Found on a variety of websites as an uncredited joke. For example: (http://jokes.cc.com/funny-kids/8d8d5k/strawberry-manure) accessed 6/16/2015.

18 Catherine Marshall, *Adventures in Prayer* (New York: Ballantine Books, 1975), 71, author's paraphrase.

19 Found on a variety of websites and considered a "mountain tale." For example: (http://www.boyscouttrail.com/content/story/falling_rock-1477.asp), accessed 6/14/2015, paraphrased.

20 Words by Edward Mote, "The Solid Rock," 1834. First appeared in Mote's *Hymns of Praise*, 1836.

21 Kent Crockett, *Making Today Count for Eternity* (Sisters, OR: Multnomah Publishers, 2001) 128, author's paraphrase.

22 Words by Edward Mote, "The Solid Rock," 1834. First appeared in Mote's *Hymns of Praise*, 1836.

23 Louisa M.R. Stead, "Tis So Sweet to Trust in Jesus," 1882.

24 Dennis Swanberg, *Swan's Soup and Salad* (West Monroe, Louisiana: Howard Publishing, 1995) 21-23. Used by permission.

25 Words by Johnson Oatman, Jr., "Count Your Blessings," 1897.